WHORAXIA, LILAC & LEONINE

BY THE AUTHOR

Scaff, Gregory. *Succubus Arts*. ISBN 978-0-9970129-0-3. Cambridge, MD: Succubus Media. 2023. Print.

WHORAXIA, LILAC & LEONINE

By

Gregory Scaff

Succubus Media

Cambridge, Maryland

20SVCCVBVSMEΔIA24

Whoraxia, Lilac & Leonine

First Edition.

Copyright ©2024 by Gregory Scaff

All Rights Reserved.

ISBN: 978-0-9970129-1-0

@gregoryscaff on Twitter

Succubus Arts - Gregory Scaff on Facebook

Succubus Media on YouTube;

https://www.youtube.com/watch?v=DXbs8Pb5rvU

Printed in the United States of America

ACKNOWLEDGEMENTS

Much appreciation to James Byrne & to Professor Pagliarulo for their kind words.
Gratitude to Allen Ginsberg & to Danielle Willis for their breathtaking splendor.
Thanks to Thorndyke Harvey, RIP.

DEDICATION

Qenaĭ meinaĭ þĭzaĭ lĭuboston ad lusta.

To the woman I love & lust over, the love of my life, the blindingly sparkly Muffin,

PREFACE

This book evolved like love in spurts over decades, conceived by the obvious need to promote a more humane, sex positive culture.

Although I've incorporated minimal prose into this work, I have chosen the elastic format of poetry to best convey my reasoning regarding consensual adult sexual behavior.

The great sexual revolution of the 1960's brought tremendous benefits to Western society but has not yet gone far enough in its cultural transformations. We live in a world where violence in media is considered more acceptable than talk of sex, the body, or desire, all of which are still disreputable, even in our porn enabled online world.

Ironically, those whose sex drives may not be as strong as others', feel compelled to be sexual because of social pressure, when sluts & celibates alike need to be cherished & not treated as aberrations.

American law has exacted considerable penalties for a variety of consensual, adult, sexual acts. After Lawrence v. Texas, 02-102 ruled in 2003 that criminal punishment for those who commit sodomy is unconstitutional, many, though not all, such laws have been expunged from the statutes.

While advances in sex positivity continue, they have also been repeatedly challenged, and even rolled back.

Recently, legal restrictions on abortion were passed in 19 states. A Texas law, SB 8, effectively bans abortions after six weeks. This draconian law not only subjects abortion providers to legal jeopardy, but also anyone who transports another to an abortion clinic in Texas. Roe v. Wade has been stricken down.

As I write this, two proposed bills in the Florida state legislature, HB 1557 & SB 1834, seek to inhibit all classroom discussion of sexual orientation or gender identity in grade schools, effectively erasing LGBTQ history, existence, & identity.

I hope that my work will add a compassionate momentum towards an indispensable, sex positive future.

It seemed fitting that I include snippets of a language called Taazhpuur that I constructed.

Goldfish to my critics, the depth of your venom only illustrates the validity of the need.

Kindness, consent & respect.

Gregory Scaff,
BeNoBou,
Maryland. 2024

KISS ME

PANEGYRICS FROM THE WHORAX

Whore: 1) One who exchanges sex for money. 2) One perceived as promiscuous, a slut.

The Lorax: a book by Dr. Seuss in which environmental activism is personified by the Lorax, who speaks for the trees in a period of ecological ick.

Whoraxia, Lilac & Leonine, the timeless & hoary home of the Whorax.

Sha nagba imuru

Those who see all, even unto the void

Gilgamesh

ᚨᚾᚨSTO𐌳EÏNS
ANASTODEINS
Anas-toth-eens

From the Gothic;
A beginning; the beginning.

First principles; the first heroic imagining, the first handshake with admitted Desire, the
first trembling touch of transcendence & carnal virtue.
Whorax Red Hilda skaun Ïst, skaun ist,
is beautiful.

YOU KNOW THIS

    Long ago
    in Africa
    we shared
    a womb
    you & I

  you know this

      you—
  simian reader
    my twin.

ALL OF ME

All of me is me indivisible, mind & body as above, so below; let sing my loins of unison like that eternal tree, whose buxom roots burrow throughout Andromeda's intemperate soul & whose decadent branches clutch tight the engorged flames of tomorrow's dawn, for see? There, there I am, Homo sapiens bodacious, that is us.

NOVEMBER DAYS

There are those November days at thirteen o'clock when we courageously overturn our awkwardness & stand-up shouting, "Hello! Look at me! Look at who I am beneath the mask! This is me!" Our loved ones will either love us or attack us, or worse, they won't even notice. Being ignored is the most benign, yet the most excruciating of sufferings one can expect, yet we cannot let this chilling dread wall us in. There are days like this, when leaves fall & Hope & Loss float upon the air, languidly embracing.

MOUNTING THE VERDANT AIRS OF IMMINENCE

Cocks-deep within the affable tranquility
Of Kindness, I sit here beloveds, floating
Like a nubile surprise rolled in carpet,
Combing through the devotion juices in
My beard while drinking my morning
Kumis & curried coffee, fantasizing
About your & Red Hilda's upcoming
Honeymoon caresses.

You are astonishing as always.
Well.
That cat is out of the bag.

Naked I waved at tour boats just like Anne*,
Rebel with a cause,
Come Freya—
I pull the pin & throw it;
Read on & do the same.

*Anne Sexton, <u>Angel of Beach Houses and Picnics</u>

THE SURVIVAL OF EROS

THE SURVIVAL OF EROS

Only now we begin to emerge from a long night of brutality, where sexual nonconformists have been subject to the utmost of religious, legal & social opprobrium.
I sought to convey through my art the utter maleficence of this terrible reality.
I hunted in garbage cans & in dumpsters for suitable ingredients with which to construct my allegory; I found a doll, a board, a feather, & a long nail.
I impaled the board, a painted panel, & the doll with the nail to convey sadistic truth. I ripped the doll's clothing, placed duct tape over the mouth, & added the feather to the hair as an emblem of innocence & individuality.
Finally, I drenched the sculpture in human menstrual blood to complete the semblance of violation. The whole was subsequently sealed against smell & decay & was then framed.
I had earlier tapped a female image as a stand-in for Humanity, an idea which seems logical to me; my painting DNA does the same.
I titled my creation The Survival of Eros in Occidental Theology as a caustic understatement regarding the dehumanized "survival" of sexual outlaws in Western civilization.
It had been common throughout Western history for certain adult consensual sex acts to be capital offenses; or punished by law with castration, mutilation, or prison, punishments at times worse than that meted out for murder.
Nazi Germany displayed a common experience of sex; jail or kill the differently sexual. Gay men were sent to the death camps for liking their own gender. Prostitute women were sent to & were forced to build Auschwitz. These women were also made to wear flimsy evening gowns, & thus didn't survive their first winter.
Certain adult consensual sex acts were banned in the West by religious decree & were punished by a lifetime of fasting & penance for one such act.
Certain adult consensual sex acts were a cause of public shame & humiliation, & could lead to the loss of one's status, employment, family, or home. Identifying as gay, promiscuous, or kinky was sufficient reason for the state to take away one's children.
Coming out currently in America as a gay, lesbian, or bi person remains a lawful reason to lose one's job in twenty-eight states. Transpersons continue to face a disproportionate level of murder & violence, & it continues to be lawful for kink practitioners to lose both their employment & their homes in all fifty states, all for consensual adult actions done in private.
Currently, legislation regarding consensual sex remains brutal. Many jurisdictions punish rape or murder with less severity than they punish certain adult consensual sex acts.
Twenty-seven states endorse abstinence-only sex education.
No state recognizes a legal right to pleasure.
Currently, access to contraceptives, or to women's health care, faces continual legislative challenges. Roe v. Wade has been stricken down.
When sex acts are the most deliriously wonderful & innocuous of human behaviors, it remains illegal in some states to have premarital sex, to cohabit without marriage, to own or buy sex toys for personal adult gratification, or even to own erotic art.
Any expression of female desire remains a political & radical act.

The making of pornography is legal in only one state, California. Sex work is legal in certain counties in only one state, Nevada. Sex workers, exotic dancers, Adult performers, & other sexual rebels face an inordinate amount of stigma & hostility from society. Indeed, common reasons given why one should not go into these professions is society's ostracism, that one will be forever unemployable. Serial killers have deliberately targeted sex workers with the belief that no one cares about them. Society's hatred for & violence against sexual dissenters does not seem to abate.

Around the world, some areas have legalized same-sex love or marriage & have given needed protections to sexual minorities & to sex workers. Sexual nonconformists, however, are still the victims of draconian & capital punishment in other countries & suffer murder rates that could be defined as genocide if an ethnic or religious group were targeted.

Despite all of this, coming out now in America as gay, lesbian, or bi is no longer a lawful reason to lose one's job in twenty-two states. The U.S. Supreme Court has upheld a right to privacy stemming from principles found in the Constitution. The watching of pornography by adults is legal in all fifty states, though state laws vary. Contraception, divorce, premarital sex, & same-sex marriage are legal.

Husbands may no longer legally rape their wives in all states. Twenty-three states reject abstinence-only sex education. Women can now retain their jobs even though they may be pregnant. Spectator sex is a legal hobby in certain jurisdictions.

Naturists, the LGBTQI community, furries, the kinky, polyamorists, sex workers, sufferers of HIV, & the Adult industry are all out & advocate for their civil & human rights. Society is more body positive & sex affirming.

We begin to emerge; first principles, ΑΝΑΣΤΩΣΕΪΝΣ, Anastodeins.

Bring on the next erotic revolution.

SKIN CARDS, BECAUSE SKIN IS IN

I like postcards; they have a physical reality. We live in an increasingly digital age, where fewer & fewer people write snail mail; thus, a postcard is rarer & even more noticeable, they have an impact. Even those who don't collect postcards often keep the cards they receive.

Because of an unexpected, front-line experience with body hatred, I created a website called SkinCards to promote sex & body positivity, social justice & culture change. The premise was simple; I would solicit or make postcards, then distribute them in bulk for others. I asked only for donations & for money to cover postage.

Currently, the sight of the scantily clad is ubiquitous, used in ads to sell beer & soap & motor oil. That is the niche; skin, & usually only pretty skin, "belongs" in media, but not in normal human actuality on the bus or in a bank.

All of us are exquisitely multidimensional. I wanted to normalize, at least in a small way, the sight of skimpily dressed real people encompassing a variety of genders, ethnicities & body shapes within a public setting.

I asked adult friends for pictures of themselves. I also advertised.

My ads ran: "Do you have bikini, bathing suit, or nude photos, which you'd like made into postcards? Do you have such postcards, or are you a business with extra promotional cards? Mail them in an envelope to me & I will make them available to others."

I then made postcards out of the contributed photos, including a spiffy nude of myself. I posted on the website: "What can you do with these postcards? Take notes on them. Mail them. Use them as Thank You cards, as party invites, leave them in hotel rooms, pin them on walls. Join me in exposing people to normalcy, in the hopes of achieving social change & a more tolerant civilization."

The impetus for this body positive advocacy began after I'd mailed beach postcards of both males & females in bathing suits to folks I knew in snowy NE from my hometown of Clearwater, Florida. Each of them expressed indignation that I had sent "naked pix" or "porn" to them. These friends worried that postal workers or neighbors would think them to be lechers or perverts; interestingly, none threw out the offensive cards.

This is because the verbalization of enjoyment of human pulchritude in our society is generally the domain of the vulgar & the disreputable. Despite all the attention paid to the human figure in media, our culture views human bodies as worthy of shame & disgrace, an attitude which I see unmistakably as an illness, a putrefaction that festers at the core of American society.

Human appearance does not, of course, equal human value. However, human beauty is one of the many pleasures of life, one which has the potential to transport & to elevate. There should exist no shame in the delight of human beauty.

Models in bathing suits are neither naked nor porn but are street legal in all fifty states. To those who complain about a surfeit of scanty imagery, I respond that if postcards of folks in bathing suits are a source of shame & outrage, then clearly, what is needed is even more postcards of folks in bathing suits.

I argue that non-sexual public nudity falls under the heading of "normal"; to that end, I included nude postcards in my project. Yes, there are naked postcards of me out there somewhere.

With the advent of email, interest eventually petered out, causing Skin Cards to go on hiatus. I moved on to other forms of sex-positive advocacy.
Spread the skin.

JACK & JILL WENT UP THE HILL: PLEASURE FOR SOCIAL PROGRESS

I have long been inspired by Dr. Susan Block, author of <u>The Bonobo Way</u>, and of Brenda Leow Tatelbaum, publisher of a long-ago erotic & progressive newspaper titled *Eidos*, by her insight for & advocacy of a need for sexual change.

Intimacy is a human need, not an option. "The needs of the people must be met," philosopher Abbie Hoffman once wrote, a statement that still resonates with me. So, in early 2004, I tried to start a masturbation club to further my Sex Radical politics.

I planned gatherings similar to what are commonly called Jack & Jill Off parties. Where mine differed from J & J parties—usually the domain of straight twenty-somethings—is that these would be places where any adult, of any persuasion, of any age, could join, masturbate, watch others masturbate, socialize, & in general, have a good time. Perhaps there would be a potluck. The one requirement was that all needed to be respectful & kind to one another.

Why masturbation? Because it is the ultimate in safe sex, free of any risk for STDs, & free of any & all social entanglements. I knew that concerns of embarrassment, self-consciousness, &
vulnerability would be raised but hoped that the benefits would outweigh initial discomfort.

Punk rockers I knew extolled solo sex in efforts to destigmatize it. Some feminists argued for masturbation as an emblem of female empowerment. Personal independence resides at the tip of a vibrator; as Madison Young says, "Every orgasm is its own revolution..." I thought of my masturbation club as pleasure for social change, for sexual revolution.

In the course of my life I have known many sexually isolated individuals. I knew that there were people who rarely, if ever, experienced intimacy—folks who were awkward, or differently abled, folks who endured years without. There were also those who were in-between partners, or those whose professional lives inhibited romance, or those for whom sex was too messy & dangerous; a reality for others, but not for them.

I reasoned that, for these folks & for others, the quality of their lives might improve if they could go to a safe, nonjudgmental, place to get themselves off, while others were getting off. I believe every town needs a culturally accepted, safe area in which adults can meet to have sexual encounters; this would provide a much-needed emotional resource for many & would potentially stave off the increasing sense of isolation & alienation that pervades contemporary society. I felt that this was a social necessity. My masturbation club was to be only the first step towards wider pleasure activism.

I spread the word about the club by inviting friends & acquaintances.

I posted fliers announcing, "JOIN A COED MASTURBATION PARTY!"

I placed ads which read: "FLYING SOLO? WHY GO IT ALONE? Think outside the box. Be the first on your block to join the new, adult, coed, solo group for women and men, couples and singles, in a safe, friendly and supportive environment."

Of the dozens who called, the most common reaction was one of doubt & disbelief that such parties could ever work. I explained that Jack & Jill Off parties met in other cities, & had done so for years, most notably in San Francisco & Orlando.

More than a few callers were surprisingly hostile, I was yelled at & berated about what a stupid idea this all was.

I wondered why someone would answer a flier or ad about an event just to say that such could never happen. I wondered too why some of them were so enraged by the idea; I could only conclude that their anger stemmed from considerable solo shame.

Also, the majority said they'd never go to a masturbation club if there were gay men there, while others asserted that they'd go only if it were for men exclusively. I explained that my vision for this was for any respectful adult, period, without barriers. I wanted to overcome socially acceptable romantic prejudices such as stigma against weight or race or age or income or social status. I clarified that I would not give in to homophobia, nor narrow the party only for gay men.

One sole woman offered to join, (Thank you Brigitte Suicide,) but only if another woman were present; I assured her that I was trying.

After multiple ads & fliers, after months of effort, I had the tiniest nucleus for a party, three men, (plus me), & the lone woman. Sadly, this wasn't enough. My insistence that the club not split between gays & straights meant that no one else joined. I did not find a second interested woman. Burned out, I stopped looking, & the club never became.

Masturbation clubs are a necessity for millions. One day places or groups like I've described will be commonplace—must be commonplace—in every town, in every city.

This is up to you.

CAPTAIN TEACH

TOO MUCH ICK

Cunt! Darkie! Fag! Slut! Kike! Whore! Mick! Spic!
Hate speech is border-free.

ABUSE ME NOT

You can't wear that, it's too short, it's not modest, it's not proper, it's not appropriate. That doesn't sound fun, no one does that, turn on the TV. That's weird. That's unnatural. That's evil. You like that? Eww! Put that away. No one wants to see that. Shame on you! You're sick. You'll grow hairy palms. You'll go to hell. Not now, we did that last month. Have you no self-respect? We'll disown you, if… We shoot people like you where I come from. Watch out, or the rednecks will beat you up. You asked for it. You deserved it.

I never acceded to your cruel oppression, to the cancer of your tyranny; in the name of compassion, coerce me not, abuse me not, repress me not.

GRATUITOUS

Gratuitous 1) given, done, bestowed, or obtained without charge or payment; voluntary. 2) being without apparent reason, cause, or justification.*

"Gratuitous," a word never uttered about rose gardens. "No! There were too many gorgeous roses in that movie, how gratuitous!"

"Gratuitous nudity:" a phrase most often uttered by ascetics who fear that there is too much happiness in the world. Their utmost concern is that someone might disparage them if they don't condemn, because their self-esteem rests upon staying aloof from the world & its gifts, because detachment equals superiority. These unfucking shits are a blight upon Humanity.

*https://www.dictionary.com/browse/gratuitous?s=t 2019.

DIAGNOSTIC CRITERIA FOR SEX-NEGATIVE GRINCHS

If it is a contest of winners & losers, of taking, of I can't believe she let him do that to her
If furry or kinky or fetish are all synonyms for weirdo crazy
If you think two genders are carved in stone
If you think that straights & gays & etc. would all be happier if they just stuck to their own kind
If it's best to do it in the dark so you don't have to see them
If you think a woman in a miniskirt in summer waiting at a bus stop with bags full of groceries is clearly a whore
If you think a boy must be gay if he does not like sports
If you're in an art gallery & interpret a passing compliment to a painting of a mermaid as some odd kind of horny come-on
If you think two men or two women kissing is unnatural & repulsive
If you need to leave the beach because a woman 100 yards away is too intimidating
If you don't masturbate because it defiles you
If you think people who have been trafficked deserve it because they are dirty
If you say that a man on the prowl is boys will be boys, but a similar woman is a tramp
If you believe missionary is the only position
If you think that a chick who says yes is a slut whom you should dump after fucking
If any remark about the attractive hair of a pedestrian is again interpreted as some odd kind of horny come-on
If you think every naturist resort is orgy central
If you're a man who wants to date lesbians because, well, two women!
If you think the horrors of Schizophrenia or HIV are justified curses from God for deviant sin
If you are gay but think the kinky are perverts; if you are kinky but think the gays are perverts;
If you believe sex is just for procreation
If you think all porn actors & prostitutes are dumb addicted & unemployable failures who recklessly spread disease to decent folks
If it's ok to show eviscerations & beheadings on television but not a woman's nipple
If the idea of staying in the same room with a dildo makes you break out in a cold sweat
If you think a normal woman is insatiable in bed but represses herself everywhere else
If news reports of missing sex workers are beneath your notice
If you think that "bisexual" is a term for those confused scaredy cats afraid to escape the closet
If you think that sexual experimentation is just an immature phase
If you think it's bad to like sex too much
If you say porn is low class & worthless
If a mother feeding her baby in public is indecent
If human genitals are gross & better never ever mentioned by name
If you think films showing intermingled consensual adults lead to rapine & death
If you think Sexologists research sex because they are just not getting any themselves
If a large hot dog causes you undue stress
If these, then unholy sex-negative Grinchdom might be yours

GIVE US YOUR TIRED, YOUR POOR*

Give us your tired, your poor, but not your really tired or really poor. Give us no wretched refuse, no one marketed, no one yearning to breathe free.

Amerikkka the land of the free & home of the conformist back in 1903 barred Anarchists, street walkers & the homeless from entering the fatherland;

Then, in order to improve WASP genetics in 1907, Social Darwinists sought to weed out the nation's criminals, the feeble minded, & the poor by introducing them to the glories of involuntary sterilization; our eugenicists cheerfully designed the first gas chambers to euthanize the unfit;

When "unfit" & "feeble minded" often meant unwed mothers, the slutty, the ethnic, or the whores, laws which lingered till 1979;

Canada passed its own Sexual Sterilization Act; Sweden forcibly sterilized those women thought to be overly sexual into the 1970's; others too, vaulted down that dank sewage pipe, like Germany, that once-sunny Weimar star, which tracked Amerikkka balls to the wall in 1933;

When the Reich prioritized its first eugenic erasures by rounding-up the homeless & the whores & the same-sex gents to be the inaugural guests for a sparkly new rehab at Auschwitz, which featured castration therapy, Herr Vivisection Doktors, & euthanasia;

No one contested this dry run for bigger things, because no one dares when no one cares;

Because, double-speak of space odyssey social design while expunging the rebel sexual; Because of the underlying ever-hate; first shame, then hysterectomies & finally cattle cars;

Because the Right pulls the conversation into the end zone, uncontested by an embarrassed Left;

Because one for all, or else division & conquest.

*from *New Colossus* by Emma Lazarus

SMOTHERINGS

We have lived for so long under the boot that we do not recall what Normal is like.

Normal is when all adults are valued equally high; Normal is the ERA; Normal is when all children are loved & educated regardless of parts or of predilections;

Normal is when law makers do not dictate the kind or amount of satisfaction desirous grownups can privately enjoy;

Normal is when we adults, with other consenting adults, can legally hold hands in public; or legally flirt in public or kiss for more than a finite time; or purchase dildos or vibrators;

Or ask another of the same gender out for a drink; or share intimacy, love & marriage, regardless of anatomy or number; or carry a box of condoms; or expose a navel on television;

Or undress while dancing for an ecstatic crowd; or model at a live art class; or own more than a set number of sex toys; or frolic alone on a computer; or view the locked-away art of Pompeii;

Or amble bare-assed to the store; or skinny dip; or create naked artwork; or hang lingerie on a clothesline where others might see; or teach human sexuality;

Or immigrate as a sex worker or a homosexual to the gold paved avenues of America that Lady Liberty so proudly offers to others;

Or blow or lick someone; or pole dance on corners for tips while street legal in a bikini; or display nudity on a billboard; or breastfeed a hungry child anywhere;

Or dance burlesque; or romp with our lovers while yet unmarried; or dress in clothing not of our prescribed gender; or watch pornography or star in it or even sell it to another;

Or do oral or anal or doggy-style, or engage in wild interracial sex; or insert several eager units into one orifice; or give or receive an enthusiastic spanking;

Or partake of BDSM fun; or pop knobs for cash; or work as a sex performer; or teach others about abortion or birth control or sex work or polygamy;

Normal is when all of these laws are over-thrown & we can legally do these things with societal approval & without police intervention, without fear of death or jail or castration or detention camps; Normal is when society persecutes no one for consensual grownup play;

Normal is when no one loses their jobs or homes or community because of their sexuality; when no one fears acid attacks from passersby, when no one fears rape, or violence, or even murder from their own families;

Normal is when women no longer suffer society's wrath & humiliation for their attire; Normal is when short skirts are a right not a request;
Normal is when tyrannical laws no longer punish women for appearing like a cop's idea of a hooker, when fishnet goths or trailer park goddesses or leather & lace punk rockers are not imprisoned for their style;

Normal is when we can publicly say the words "leg" or "arm," or the names for any body part without social reprobation;

Normal is overthrow the Patriarchy; Normal is overthrow the Matriarchy; Normal tosses these to sewage tanks & lexicographers.

Normal is when all bodies are celebrated & adored; is when all genitalia are valued as is & are neither circumcised, nor surgically altered, nor are sewn shut or otherwise mutilated;

Normal is when sexuality is nurturing & respectable & spiritual & affirmative & artistic & does not co-opt intelligence; Normal is when sexuality does not come with a bull's eye; Normal is groping yourself; Normal is bloody every month; Normal is sex as art;

Normal is a united kinky, vanilla, furry, fetish & pan-sexual community; Normal is the skilled & dignified creativity of sex work; Normal is a whore is a whore is a human being, some-one's beloved child;

Normal is when grown-ups possess the inalienable right to pursue love, passion & marriage; to learn, to express their thoughts & to advocate for their erotic freedoms; Normal is virginity; is monogamy; Normal is many, successively or all at once; Normal is The Bonobo Way;

Normal is when we become the shameless erotic sovereigns we evolved to be, when lust shimmers from the very protons of our being like a wondrous halo of iridescent animal light, without shame or embarrassment & as safely as eating cheese;

Normal is when no one blinks because you're a southpaw, or are from Burma, or have green eyes, or five fingers, or are nude in public, or if you like bagels with olives & peanut butter, or if you consummate others for a living, or if you are kinky or queer or poly;

Normal is when it doesn't matter how many lovers one has or what gender they must be, because we're all just wonderful people, worthy of respect & civility, who shop at the mall & live next door.

STELE OF THE STRANGLED & BURIED IN A DUMPSTER

"Dr. Guerin...succeeded in curing young girls of the vice of onanism by burning the clitoris with a hot iron."
Onanisme *Avec Troubles Nerveux Chez Deux Petites Filles*
Dr. Demetrius Zambaco, 1882

Remember the lack of Normal & our bare survival.

Remember the scholarly words of Time, that conscientious full-grown mingling, regardless of categories, or of methods, entrances, or attire, causes no harm to the commonweal.

Remember the Puritan decorum of impoverished austerity; Comstock's many-bannered Morlocks at war amongst themselves & against all, who are alike in their absexual venom by claiming that we are unclean abominations deserving of flogging or prison or the auto-da-fé;

Remember that most sex acts have been closeted & illegal;

Remember the fasting & the prayers, the forced binary, the hidebound stereotypes; remember the hushed voices & the humiliation, the unspoken judgements & the cranial straitjackets; remember the censorship, the blurred-out parts & the hidden cabinets;

Remember that Soviets & Americans both purged homosexuals during the Cold War;

Remember the Toronto Barracks Raid of 1978;

Remember CBS' lurid "documentary" Gay Power, Gay Politics, an agitprop tool for the Religious Right which presented hatred & gossip as fact;

Remember Mike Diana, the only American artist convicted of Obscenity for his underground paintings, because to criticize society & religion threatens the entrenched old regime; rock on, Mike;

Remember the malevolent, governmental nonchalance that fueled the AIDS epidemic; remember, "silence = death"; remember the hiding & the isolation, the outed banishment from kith & kin, the bullying & rapes & assaults, the lobotomies, the Thorazine, the penitentiary; remember Stonewall, remember Pulse, remember Harvey Milk;

Remember that Death rides a shamed horse; remember that "Old Fashioned" is for the timid & stomped upon;

Remember the unheralded deviants & prostitutes, hunted down by law to be forcibly sterilized;

Remember the belittling stigma concerning female lust, the disgust at those who shared their desires, at those who dared initiate sex;

Remember the women cured of their cravings by the mandated slicing away of their clitoris, or by the amputation of their wombs; remember the loose women who fucked for the non-commercial bliss of it, yet were locked up as whores for avid & adult, "indiscriminate sex";

Remember the harassment; the panic to not resemble a slut; remember the deadly reviling of Jezebels & triple X'rs; remember Lenora Frago, legally murdered for not putting out;

Remember Jack the Ripper & the Green River Killer & their Red Light slasher friends who puke their merciless hatred upon women & night walkers, the forgotten & ignored, who are not seen until their corpses rain from the heavens & society cannot breathe for the stench that it has caused;

Remember the Magdalene Home labor camps for the professional, the masturbatory, the amorous over-achievers or the merely too pretty, expected possibly someday to plummet into sin; all incarcerated, tortured, & enslaved;

Remember the rubber enthusiasts, the transpersons, the leather kinky, the ménage à hundred; remember the courtrooms & the psych evals, the lost careers & child custody, the destitution, the ostracism & the blame;

Remember Kenneth Appleby, an adult sent to the slammer for ten years for gently thwacking the bottom of his wanting adult gay lover with a riding crop;

Remember the unfucking model rags & their fur ball propaganda, the Dachau dieting, death march starvation of millions—the murderous, self-imposed anorexia of innocents—the gaunt ideals of a merciless for-profit fashion;

Remember the burning cross terrorisms, the clothes hangers, the abortion clinic bombings, the assassinations, the kidnappings, the death threats, the bomb threats, the arsons, the vandalism;

Remember our dead, the "honor" killings, the lynched & the executed, too many to name;

Remember the black triangle women deemed asocial rubbish & euthanized or spayed or packed into cattle cars to their deaths; remember the pink triangle men tossed away;

Remember the National Socialists, for they came for you before they went for them; Remember, & never go back.

TERRORISM IN THE U.S.A.

Remember that American terrorists threaten to kill doctors, nurses, & women;
Remember that American terrorists murder abortion providers;
Remember that American terrorists bomb abortion clinics;
Remember that American terrorists can be devout who choose to murder;

Remember that American terrorists assault, rape & murder prostitutes;
Remember that the media colludes at times with American terrorists by printing no mention of prostitute deaths;
Remember that police collude at times with American terrorists by not investigating the murders of prostitutes until the bodies pile too high to escape;
Remember that American terrorists can be serial killers who prey on the reviled of America;

Remember that American terrorists assault & murder gay/bi/lesbian/intersexed & transgendered people;
Remember that American terrorists assault & murder people of color;
Remember that American terrorists assault & murder Jews;
Remember that American terrorists can be Christians, nationalists & white supremacists.

Remember that American terrorist laws rarely focus on everyday terrorism in America.

STYLITES & MIRRORS, AMERICAN SEX

"You are gorgeous Queen 'tis true—
but sweet Snow White is hotter than you."

I

"Lust is infidelity,
& infidelity lust,
gouge it out. *

abandon marriage,
castration is better. **

burn the clit,
cure masturbation: ***"

we are the ones
whom the gods wish to
destroy.

II

Muffled screams
& a naked form;
a mossy slab;
thirteen black robes,
thirteen black candles,
a Black Mass;
new moon shadow &
shivering light.

They had snatched her,
had taken Snow White
from her beloveds,
had stripped her, spread her,
chained her across
a chilled & damp rock.

Jangling shackles,
arced out flesh,
bruised & quivering;
whimpering, cyanotic;
locked & broken eyes,
a punched & bleeding

slit, Host defiled;
coerced & night-frigid
tips; grim the High Priest
pondered the pale display.

Began the cleric,
"Abyssus abyssum invocat,
Ave Satanas!"

"Hell calls to Hell," echoed
the grotto, "Hail Satan!"

"Domine Satanas, Rex
Infernus, Imperator
omnipotens nobis vocamus,"

"Lord Satan, King of the
Underworld, omnipotent
Emperor, we invoke you."

A stained ivory bowl
raised high, a carved
human skull, graveyard
robbed upon the thirteenth
night, upon a full moon,
brimful with the crusted
black blood of a slaughtered
black cat; a black goat's
tail dipped & spattered
across the reviled innocent.

"Offerimus tibi
Domine Satanas,
calixem voluptatis
etenim carnis accipiam,"

"O' Lord Satan,
accept our foul gift
of fleshly desire."

A Damascened blade
from velvet cape, plunged
directly & without
culpability
between silken pink,
plowing up slowly

& deliberately
through the navel unto
the last thump of the
heart; a blood-spitting
howl falling hoarsely,
finally, into crickets.

The sign of Baphomet,
the sodden Host, pulled
out & passed around.
Waving aloft the
human switchblade,
victorious the
High Priest shouted;

"Ecce calix voluptatis
carnis, et fac altare
sceleratis Domini
Inferi, Satane vivet!
Ave Satanas!"

"Behold, the carnal
chalice of lust. Make
Unholy the altar
of the Lord of the
Underworld.
Satan lives!
Hail Satan!"

Drumming the savaged
woods, hatchets & daggers
hacked off, peeled off;
plucking out the
anthropological
& "libertine" Snow
White like so much
misanthropy pâté.

III

Custom & law,
get thee behind me.
Mrs. Grundy Stars & Stripes,
finite your landscape, cold;
what shame,
what denunciations,

what discord;
pogroms & malice
& razor wire, lifespans
lost under the bed.

* Matthew 5:28-29
** Matthew 9:12
*** *Onanisme Avec Troubles Nerveux Chez Deux Petites Filles*. Demetrius Zambaco, 1882.

SPELLBOUND

The campfire twisted in the writhing wind, glimmering the dancers' comforting flanks like delicious & rippling coals. In a pine bough harmony of beguiling chants the Singer of Bygone Things released the euphoric antiquities.
Pop. Boom sticks kaboomed. Phrenologists stepped out uninvited from the forest & pointed their sticks & whomever they pointed at died in spurts of blood. Pop.
Naked I stood, tied to a tree on a mound of logs, gawking speechless at the jeering mob, the hangman, watching the faces whom I had loved glide across the everlasting screen. Pop.
Night cradled me as I wept.
Frïaþwa, duhʋe uns bïlaïþ? Friathwa, duhve uns bilaith?
Love, why have you forsaken us?
Fallen from the heavens to flee beneath the Basento, I sobbed my aching tears in a gust of ash like vindictive feathers that first pulsed deafeningly, painfully, then ever, ever quieter unto whispers & hoarfrost, oh Laika. Pop.
They hunt us for sport; they say slaughter is a kind of cleansing. Pop pop pop. They say we taste like pork. They

SUI JURIS COURAGE NECESSARY

Willing, Epicurean, hedonistic.
Pleasure-loving, self-indulgent:

Convulsive happiness, unabashed ecstasy,
Exultation, gut-wrenching ferocity,
Euphoria, Orgies of delight,
Bacchanalias of yearning sensation:

Alluring, curvaceous, slinky, sultry, stacked,
Busty, built, full-figured, shapely.
Womanly:

Innocuous words wreathed in damnation to
Scorn the Only in the National Geographic;

Ascetic proxy for promiscuous, lascivious,
Immoderate; for slut, harlot, whore:

Heed your primal calling, Humanity,
Only in the National Geographic.

NON-PERMISSION

In the echoing vacuum of a
Collective Yes
There dwells an angry No;
A lonely null and void, where
Once cheerful, tail-
Wagging sex becomes
One-sided fencing &
Like all Felonious Assaults
Devolves into cruel trauma
& merited jail.

"Never marry a Lombard
Woman, they smell*."

*Einhard to Charlemagne.

PSYCHOPATHIA SEXUALIS

In a moon-perky time of rose blossoms
& barbecue, when hooking-up drifted
In the air like erectile cologne, a
Commonplace man mundane in his irritations
Shopped at a bear bar for a voluptuous
Tryst, a boozy rendezvous which gifted
Him both redemption & delirium
Between a silver pick-up & a Chevy
Tahoe.

While still prick-out, revulsion rose caustic
In his throat like a cloak of battery
Acid tossed across the optics of his
Consciousness; glowering, he bludgeoned his
Philanthropic date into the safe harbor
Of an ambulance & to the very
Gateways of Paradise, because, kill the
Fag! Kill the fag!

Oh, wait...wait.

Not appreciated, John Winthrop.

FORBIDDEN

"Since then, however, learning, with its humanizing influences, has made great progress, and morals and religion have made some progress with it. Therefore, a rod which may be drawn through the wedding ring is not now deemed necessary to teach the wife her duty and subjection to the husband. The husband is therefore not justified or allowed by law to use such a weapon, or any other, for her moderate correction. The wife is not to be considered as the husband's slave. The privilege, ancient though it may be, to beat her with a stick, to pull her hair, choke her, spit in her face or kick her about the floor or to inflict upon her other like indignities, is not now acknowledged by our law."
—Fulgham vs. the State of Alabama, 1871.

The 19th Amendment of the US Constitution
Allowed women the vote in August of 1920;
After eighteen other amendments in a
Hundred & thirty-one years;

Forty-nine years after Fulgham freed
Women from marital slavery,
Albeit not from marital rape;

Fifty-five years after Appomattox
& the 13th Amendment abolished
Slavery in the United States;

& a hundred & forty-five years after
Lexington & Concorde brought liberty
To wealthy free white guys,

As Liberty or Death smiles pungent of
Magnolia sunbeams, Thalia's saccharine
Mask of the two-faced & the tight-fisted.

CRY, LASCIVIOUS MUSE: THE PLIGHT OF A NON-MARTIAN CIS MALE

O pounding asteroids! O flashing meteors! O pink and purple horse-head nebula! O spiral galactic arms, O rich-bottomed Milky Way! O starry-eyed hand-holders! O morning park panties! O side-walk condoms! O tree-branch Trojan wrappers! O romantics sneaking off trail! O, hooray for others.

"Oh. You don't earn enough. You're...an artist. A poet. Unemployed. A pervert, an abomination, a slut. You're too fat too thin too short too young too old too weird too this too that, too too too!"

O that of distant fairytale, to greet the tiniest whiff of feminine skin! Auvernal comes our customary mold; if women truly sprang from Venus, that uber-mammalian & compulsively embracing Cytherean, then cold & discarded chastity would not confine my fate.

THE DEATH OF SLAVERY IN THE WEST

In Europe slavery officially ended when the Ottomon sultan freed his harem in 1903. However, the last legal slavery in Europe were the Magdalene Homes of Ireland. Magdalene Homes were institutions for "wicked" girls—for whores, for unwed mothers, for those who were lustful, or those unlucky to be pretty and thus more likely to fall into sin. Girls were sent to these labor camps often for life by the Catholic church in Ireland. Women were deprived of all human rights, were tortured, beaten, starved, kept locked inside by nuns, and forced to work for free. The last Magdalene Home closed on September 25, 1996, the true date of the end of legal slavery in Europe. This was only made possible because sex was considered an evil to be expunged at all costs.

Rectify the dissipated & the Jezebel,
Incarcerate the pretty before they sin.
Chastise the raped & the expecting,
Lust is wickedness & wickedness a crime.

Once upon an Ireland grim, rehab
Homes like underwear crust arose
To scrub the isle of feminine vice,
To cleanse by blood & sweat & toil;

By punishment cells, by silence, canings
& seclusion; by starvation, by shaven
Heads, ice-water baths & stripped
Humiliation; by the theft of names for

Numbers, by outlawed self-exploration,
& by work; work, washing clothes fourteen
Hours a day; work will set them free.

Wantonness merits no choice, no pay,
No mercy, for base wickedness drips
From Suffering like foul stigmata until
Pious virtue shines from fallen souls like
St. Eulalia's blessed dove.

(But only the fit depraved—the disabled
Corrupt cannot work, they're on their own.)

No epitaphs, no flowers, no lonely graves,
The government has slimed away.

Magdalene Homes, O Magdalene Homes,
With what little sorrow we mark your
Passing, on September 25, 1996.

A THREE-PART ANTHROPOLOGICAL TREATISE ON HUMAN DESIRES

Of Neandertals, Zana, & Polynesians.

I.

Many, many, befores before, back when
We were all tall, dark & Aurignacian,
We encountered those cavern trolls, those
Stubby-legged & brow-ridge people.
What clownish hair!
What fish belly skin!
What outlandish schnozzes!
They did not even roast marshmallows!

But we ignored all that, we ignored all that,
Because we peeked beneath
Their mammoth-fur loincloths,
& that we could not ignore;
We watched them deadlift
Buffaloes, & that we could not ignore.
We said, "Hey baby, step into
My tent," & they said
"I'm gonna climb you like a tree."

(These are my parents, & yours.)

II.

In 1850 Zana the ferocious wild
Woman with tremendous bazooms
Was dragged from the woods of southern Russia.
Though she fought & howled & bit, they locked her
In a cage for three years, from where the
Denigrations flew like explosive
Yersinia bumps.

Zana the ape-chick rips off all of her clothes!
Zana climbs trees like a monkey!
She is hairy as a chimp!
Zana sleeps in a hole in the ground!
She runs naked in the snow!
She can out-race horses!
Zana can carry 200 lbs.!

One handed!
Uphill!
Zana growled & grunted, but like Philomela,
Never said a word, alas.
Zana was "dirty," "ugly," "ape-like," "repellant."
Zana was not human; they branded her
a "yeti, a relic Neandertal, the Missing Link;"
Yet, & yet, Zana the ferocious ape-chick
Dropped a litter of Homo sapiens sapiens,
Which she caught when she was passed out drunk.

III.

Like those bigoted Captain Cooks who wrote
In their logs, "The natives are gruesome
In every respect, they are black & hideous,
With squished noses & bizarre appearance.
The crew has grown defiant & well nigh
Mutinous; despite threats of flogging &
Keelhauling, they continue to pull nails
From the ribs of the ship itself, in order
To pay the savages to fornicate
With them*."

*attribution unknown

REPUDIATION: EUPHEMISMS

I refuse to do the nasty, to bump uglies, to stain, to stab, to use, to have my foul way, to invade, to take advantage of, to ruin that, to do a rudeness to, to do the act of shame, to shove the devil into hell, to score between the posts, to spear the bearded clam;

To the best of my knowledge—& I have researched this often & repeatedly, but to no avail—I have no dirty parts, or naughty bits, or even secret areas;

I have never met a flytrap, an axe wound, a gash, a gutted hamster, a carnal snare, a trout, a tuna, a fishpond, a grease box, a scat, a stank, a stench, a stinkpot;

A thing, a pork sword, a bayonet, a virgin splitter, a battering ram, God's revenge on women, my enemy, a cannon, a conman, or a cunt-killer, anywhere in the esteemed pages of Gray's Anatomy, although I have examined each & every one;

Nuzzle me, lover, with a harbor of hope, a best friend, a masterpiece, a treasure, a delight, a yum-yum, a portal of Venus, a velvet underground, a jewel in the lotus, a divining rod, a lollipop, or a honeypot, you Paradise on Earth.

OR RAGNAROK

NUDA VERITAS

The nude is, after all, the most serious form of art.
—Kenneth Clark

Human beauty values
Stately, like Stonehenge
or Hamlet

Art for art's sake
Nude for nude's sake

Love for love's sake
Lust for lust's sake

Never scorn gratuitous joy

LANDSCAPES, BEAUTY'S ANTHROPOLOGIA

"The first time I saw a live naked woman I fainted, passed out on the floor."
—Anonymous

Picture your most attractive scene;
Grown-ups parade their own impressed attire,
This one snowy peaks, & that one alligator grass,
& little ones color a grassland, dotted with trees—
O lost savanna,
O extinct east Africa,
O tempestuous Mother,
How yet we mourn you!

But of Splendor's beau ideal, it is us;
The ultimate breathless pause, it is us;
The universal one for all,
Beyond all, over all; it is us.
Go now, Supernova, check the mirror
& you will see that this is true.

PRIMATE INHERITANCE

Steeped in the traditional & enduring best of chimp
Decorum, the curvaceous hunt radiates like a neon
Billboard made up of high heels, tangled hair & tie tacs,
Projecting our lust through aching cobweb searchlights.
"Hello, my name is Human, I seek a tall & limber person
Who only fucks upside down in trees, nice to meet you."
Bow-chicka-wah-wah is our middle name.

Confess, we hypocrites.

Though we hunt in the enduring best of chimp propriety,
We act as if we are all one discreet species, as if my hunt
For X & your hunt for Y & your hunt for A means that we
Cannot talk, cannot mix, cannot be seen together,
Though no one cares about your hunt for X or Y or
A when gardening, just as no one cares about your fondness
For anchovies, except when ordering pizza.

Confess, we hypocrites.

YOUR VERY LIPS MANIFESTO

The joints of your thighs are like jewels, the work of a skilled artist.
—The Song of Solomon 7:1

I.

Wind wraith sky shatter,
star anvil-clatter—luscious
your lips unself me.

Joyful you—delightful,
delectable, exhilarating!
Your liquid swayings,
those flying Romanesques!
The hypnotic ripples of
your sacred triple angles
stun me into ecstasy.

II.

Bulletproof in your beach
towel, you scrunch the six
steps from the dressing room
to the pool so no one scopes
out the searing glory of you,
promenading in wispy,
Brazilian Lycra.

You cry that this is crinkled
and that is frizzled—that
these are chunky but those are thin,
while this—this is just weird;
yet astonished passersby gape
after you, awakened by their
shamelessness into epiphany.

III.

I want to kiss your blistering
pavement Highway 19;
you 98 degree sunstroking
cloud of exhaust,

I embrace you, for along
your route hallowed Splendor
shines like Selene
in thong clad Helens from
Fairy Land, who vend
from carts that gild your
path like sparklers beneath
a diamond and cottontail sky.

How sleek and glistening you
marketeers are, with your
legs gleaming like ivory tusks,
dizzying with those amber
fields of flesh, more
gorgeous than every sunset,
more spectacular than
the Milky Way—
so persist in your coy
wiggling, oh Florida nymphs,
drown me in pulchritude—
drench me in flesh,
in the beneficence of muscle
and skin and anatomical
veracity—plunge me in
the steamy flamingo
glow of bliss,
rocket me into Elysium.

For you I am Kong howling
atop the Empire State,
I can never devour my fill.

BAYWATCH: A SAD BUT PREDICTABLE DEATH

Praises to Angelica Bridges, Nicole Eggert, Erika Eleniak, Marliece Andrada, Pamela Anderson, Yasmine Bleeth, & to Carmen Electra & others.

All that I can predict, all I know, is this, that;
If I feasted on fish tacos while strolling upon the Coppertone boardwalk of Venice Beach,
If I soaked on the palm toasty sand, if I swam in the chill waves, if a riptide sucked me out,
If whitecaps overtook me, if salt-caustic water gushed into my wretched lungs, &
If the naiad superheroes of Baywatch jet-skied over, yelling, "Give me your hand!"
Then the downy colossus of Immortal Beauty would squish my synaptic axons like amoeba slides, no handholding for you; &
Fair-cheeked Helen of a Thousand Ships would hush my Arctic syrupy veins, be still my brazen & grateful heart, what sludge, &
She would hark! The shipwrecked zeppelins of my lungs sing wantonly of drier tides, &
Like King Kong I would glide into the frosty grip of the abyss, just another notch for Davey Jones.

"Death by Human Pulchritude"
Would read my epitaph.

I offer no defense.

BIKINI WOMAN

> You sent me a postcard of a naked woman from Florida...
> —Angry ex-friends

A woman in a bikini is not
nude is not naked is
not obscene she is
clothed she is covered she
is street legal vroom vroom

see Bikini Woman amble
downtown see
her sip cappuccino
see her shop at the mall!

She is unashamed
She is unadulterated
She is Bikini Woman

You are that overwhelming;
You are that Woman.

CULTURAL OUTLAW

in the now of rugged tobacco cowboys
of sex sells & breasty beer commercials

of easy porn of tampon & condom
ads of penis pill telecasters

of Slut Walks the Lusty Lady
of COYOTE of dildo billboards

of bikini car shows
of the Free Speech Coalition

of Miracle Bra runways &
nymphet blue jean commercials

—when just to say
"I want I lust I imagine I masturbate

I have hidden the salami—
often & with many—
I have kinked I have done it for cash

I have gushed on film"
all remain a Radical act

akin to feeding the homeless
or coming out as trans

or tossing a Molotov into
the stock exchange.

Yea for human artistry
yea Amendment One

yea for quitting the shadows
yea for easy porn

yea for kindred yea for solidarity
join the outside, Spartacus—it's warmer.

WHORAX*

"Modesty is a crime; Shamelessness is a Virtue. I am the Whorax, I speak for the Sluts."
—Mazy Kyst

Dada is the tasty
cunt-dripping &
harmonic Succubus
swaggering naked
down the white lines of
Main Street at high noon
resounding her Liberty
breasts, calling out
"I am the Whorax,
bring out your sluts;
your Dachau harlots,
your money shot strumpets,
your Magdalene House
cumtwats, your retched-up
& interstitial.

*From Gregory Scaff, *Gluteal Contact Rocking Horse*, a Dada poem.

E PLURIBUS UNUM, FOR EXAMPLE

$$= > \div$$
—Graffiti, 2020

Everyone's left embraces their right; if you are furry, march on Gay Pride Day; if you are lesbian or bi or gay, defend the fetishists; if you're a fetishist, protest with the sluts; if you are a slut, stick up for the mono hets; if you are mono het, march with the sex workers; if you're a sex worker, demonstrate with the naturists; if you're a naturist, support the poly; if you are poly, uphold the kinky; if you are kinky, lobby with the trans; if you are trans, back the furries; if you are human, become the revolution.

O Erato! O Red Hilda!
Sluts unite; we are all in this together;

Come out, come out, whatever you are.

ON PRAVDA & OTHER TRADITIONAL ORGANS

Unfuck this & unfuck that & unfuck you, Cruelty,
With your inhumane modesties & your
Venomous sexual inheritances, with your T-rex
Values of "woman" & of "man," with your
Barbed wire walls that smother us all, unfuck you.

Let there be a charred layer of ash between us.

Regardless of facades or dimensions
Or other hollow vacancies,
In spite of Corporate's party line
& the jagged, alligator gar
Diktat of Little Brother,
I am the right to lust & to life,
To do or not to do;
To wear or not to wear;
To read to think to experience, to find
& define fallopial truth for myself.

I am autonomous—a human Inverted
Jenny—begotten sky-clad on Cloud
Nine, where psychic, intergalactic ravens
Nestle on my shoulders like Blackbeard
& living dead warriors feast on mead &
Bacon & clatter their battle axes in my hall.

Bare-assed & wielding rattlesnakes for
Reins, I ride a Stygian wolf through
Unmapped forests & across the moon,

I am Freydis slapping my gravid breasts
With the icy sword of a corpse while
Storming the iron gates of Valhalla.

I am Human, the only necessary motivation
the only requisite explanation
the only obligatory justification.

"Even" in fishnet, boots & a thong,
I flaunt an IQ larger than the
Library of Congress—I am
a free human—my gaze splinters cinder block,
I will gut you on your glass-ceiling
Double standards.

COME OUT COME OUT

Every blastocyst a female,
Every male of us a trans.

Gender worries are carbon-dated, transcend.
Gender & its cravings dwell in
Chemistry & not the loins;
Multiplicity reigns; no one is a Xerox.
I believe in Klein's Grid, in Kinsey's seven-
Points & the gorgeous variations therein,

I believe in bones & blood & skin & flesh,
I believe in the apposites of male & female, &
The varieties in between; in the five sexes,
In the girls who wake up one day as boys,
In the many inter ones with this & that;
I believe in discordant trans, in the breadth
Of ones too plentiful & amazing to name,
You can pee next to me.

The motherly voice of Multiplicity
Calls out to you all,
Come out come out
Whoever you are.

OUR EROTIC LEGACY, FRAGMENTS & WHISPERS

En Hedu'anna, High Priestess of the Moon God in Ur,

Sappho, Ovid, Catullus, Vatsyayana, Aristophanes, Petronius, Praxiteles, Queen Esther, Song of Solomon, Marcolf,

Rabelais, Boccaccio, Sir Francis Dashwood, Marquis de Sade, John Cleland, Leopold von Sacher-Masoch, Whitman, Swinburne, Edgar Rice Burroughs, Erica Jong, John Norman, Jennifer Blowdryer,

Magnus Hirschfeld, Susie Bright, Carol Queen, Priscilla Alexander, Nina Hartley, Betty Dodson, Megan Andelloux, Xaviera Hollander, Lee Harrington, RuPaul, Joani Blank, Louis Réard, Rudi Gernreich,

Margaret Sanger, Bill Baird, Frank Kameny, Jane Roe, Dr. Joyce Wallace,

Alexandre Jean Baptiste Parent-Duchatelet, Richard Freiherr von Krafft-Ebing, Havelock Ellis, Gräfenberg, Sigmund Freud, John Money, Masters & Johnson, Kinsey, Margaret Mead, Bronislaw Malinowski, Dr. Block, Gayle Rubin, Anne Fausto-Sterling, Helen B. Fisher, Madison Young,

Appomattox, Comstock, Stonewall, Loving v. Virginia, Star Trek, Harvey Milk, HIV, Civil Unions, Lawrence v. Texas,

The Hellfire Club, Plato's Retreat, the Eulenspiegel Society, DarkOdyssey, C.O.Y.O.T.E, The Free Speech Coalition, Eidos, SWOP USA, FEMEN, Fuck for Forest, Planned Parenthood, Woodhull Freedom Foundation, National Coalition for Sexual Freedom,

Fayaway, Lydia Thompson Burlesque, Carol Doda,

Bettie Page, Tara Alexander, Cicciolina, Annie Sprinkle, Erika Lust, Bill Osco & Howard Ziehm, Candida Royalle, Marilyn Chambers, Larry Flynt, Hugh Hefner, Bob Guccione, Brenda Leow Tatelbaum,

Urs Graf, Aretino, Bosch, Giovanni Battista Palumba, Artemisia Gentileschi, Boucher, Rubens, Bouguereau, Renoir, Modigliani, Klimt, Schiele, Irving Klaw, Lucian Freud, Mike Diana, Frazetta, Boris, Scaff,

French postcards, pillow books, Tijuana bibles, VHS, porno theaters, Paul Fussell's Category X,

Lil Johnson, Bessie Smith, The Toppers, Elvis, The Rolling Stones, Donna Summer, Madonna, the Buzzcocks, the Divinyls, the Slits, X-Ray Specs, Lady Gaga, Aaliyah, Beyoncé, Rihanna, Lords of Acid, Nicki Minaj;
Rock 'N Roll.

OF BARE SKIN & HUMAN ANASYRMAICA

Speak, bountiful Muse, of the castaway & the disappeared, hurled by harsh fate unto distant shores;*

Speak besides of that adoring baobab, of 13-Reed & the four milky streams, of the Plain of High Heaven & the Air Spirit mother, the mother of the waters; speak of the Sovereign Plumed Serpent & the broken shell;

"In the downy & ovarian Dreaming of once upon & faraway, you scavenged across the mammoth veld, brandishing jagged rocks in battle with scimitar cats & short faced bears, naked you lived & naked you died;

With your own sun-robed legacy I gift you, with skin's ever-belonging I goad you, hear the disremembered yesterdays; the festive hunter-gatherer altogetherness, the woven hats & frond sandals; the g-strings, the fox tails, the bone & teeth necklaces, the tassel of moss wrapper for your Ginnungagap; the loincloths, from Oldowan to Mouse;

Hark, the Occidental skin; the longhaired & bear-caped warriors, the liberate-the-nipple string skirts, the horse pizzle of Frey, the twat-wide Sheelas above the door;

The hothouse blossoms of Sydon & of Tyre, the civilizing cum shots of the West; the Minoan breasts, the Egyptian faïence bead & fishnet dresses,

The beloved Priapus at the park; the foreskin Magna Graecia, the oiled up, naked to the glans Olympics, the nymphs above the couch, the au naturel market-stall Cynics, the Pan decor of altars & of coffee shops, the scruffy nudity of Toiling Peasant Everyone;

Genitalia protected; nudity embodied Deity.

Hear, that a woman sans useless add-ons is not only fabulous, but was sacred & powerful, an anasyrmaic & exorcismic Boudicca on the half-shell who quelled lightning bolts & hurricanes, who saved us all from that which growls in the night, the Marianne at the boar's snout bringing deliverance & restoration;

Hear, that chimney sweeps & monarchs wore charms of flying wands & winged vulvas; love muscles were apotropaic haute couture. How cool is that? Just keeping a twat shot in your wallet could win you the lottery!

& lo, I give you corner cocks. Balls-deep phalluses with ripply marble veins once brought fertility & fortune on urban boulevards, they were out, they were up & they were proud! "Buff me baby, I give good luck; lean on me, I'm here for you until your bus comes!"
Venerate your ecdysiast heritage, my hominin & Keko Mask sybarites."

*To Erato, *The Odyssey* 1:1

VESICA PISCIS: VENNS

Arapesh Mundugumor Tschambuli Matrilocality Patrilocality Matrifocality Exogamy Endogamy Co-Marriage Ghost Marriage Cross Cousins Levirate Sororate Incest Taboo

Sexual Dimorphism Fourth Gender Gender Role Berdache Serial Monogamy Polyandry Polygamy Polygyny Purdah Sexual Terrorism;

Sacrum Femur Gluteus Maximus Mons Veneris Labia Minora Vulva Vagina Clitoris Cervix Vas Deferens Glans Penis Corpora Cavernosa Testes Seminal Vesicles;

Limbic Brain Neurons Dopamine Hypothalamus Oxytocin Limerence Love Passion; Us;

Anthro Anthropomorphic Furry Fursona Fursuit Furmeet Furotica Netfur Fanfic Yiff Spooge Paw Off Scaly Avie Kitsune Were Otherkin Therian Therianthrope Mundane;

Ha A Tey Ze Hir Mx. Transsexual FTM MTF Transition Transgender Transphobia Transmurder Remembrance Day;

Top Bottom Kink R.A.C.K. S.S.C. Safe Word BDSM Masochism Venus in Furs Domina de Sade Single Tail Flogger Fetish Latex

Pony girl Plushy Paleophilia Hamrosophilia Ecosexual;

Two Spirit Mahu Bitesha Enaree Transvestite Drag Queen Crossdress;

Skiing Solo Boy-Girl Jackhammer DP Reverse Cowgirl Money Shot Gonzo XXX AVN Blue;

Herms Merms Ferms Third Gender, Fifth Gender Guevedoce DSD Gender Variant Intersex Non-binary Skoliosexual;

Swinging Open Marriage Group Monogamy Metamour Mono-poly Poly Polyfidelity Triad Quad;

Coming Out Genderqueer Lipstick Lesbian Butch Femme Homosexual Bi Bicurious Bigender Bi- phobia LGBTQI Gender Non-Conforming Gender Identity

Gender Expression Gender Fluid Cisgender Feminine Presenting Masculine of Center Heterosexism;

Black Red Purple Dark Aesthetic Dark Arts Gothic Pale Bettie Bangs Mohawks Spiked Leather Ragged Bras Fishnet & Boots Punk Rock Bauhaus Dracula Blood Fetish Handcuffs;

Tricks Dates Transactional Sex Call Girl Escort Streetwalker Whore Courtesan Sex Worker Madam Brothel Cathouse Red Light Roses Donations The Works Half & Half BBBJ;

Third Base French Groping Cuddling Honesty Communication XOXO & Firkytoodle;

Yes yes O yes & a cigarette, & more.

FAH NAHT, CARPE NOCTEM, SIEZE THE NIGHT

Fah naht.
"Matjam jah drïgkam,
unte du maurgïna gaswïltam."

Fah naht.
"Matjam jah drigkam,
unte du maurgina gaswiltam."

"Eat, drink & party on,
for tomorrow we may die."

Seize the night, rub the lamp, free
The skin, release the PDAs!

Live now, love now, respect
Now, in the morning & forever after.

The Reaper lost his phone & never calls ahead,
So rude.

LE CADAVRE EXQUIS BOIRA LE VIN NOUVEAU

"The exquisite corpse shall drink the new wine."

Hark, the wrath of outcasts & of street corner harbingers
Rebellion & Lust will merge beauteous upon my lap,
Chiming down Parliament like phoenix church bells.
Standing up for "I Desire" becomes the dawn—my family,
My selves, my born from the ashes.

THANKSGIVINGS

O Juli Ashton! Nina Hartley! Tom Byron! Shanna McCullough! Asia Carrera! Peter North! Sydney Steele! Brittany O'Connell! Serenity! Janet Jacme! Jewel De'Nyle! Sasha Grey! Sunny Lane! Justine Joli! Debi Diamond!

O Claire Adams! Flower Tucci! Puma Swede! Lexington Steele! Kylie Ireland! Raylene! Lizzy Borden! Buck Angel! Taylor St Claire! Tasha Voux! Kaitlyn Ashley! Joanna Angel! Strokahontas! Mazy Kyst! Midnight Play! Evan Stone! Savannah Sly! Alexandria Quinn! O Freya!

Gratitude upon gratitude upon gratitude.

UFKUNNAÏ ÞUK SÏLBAN, UFKUNNAI THUK SILBAN*

Grab a box of nails & a claw hammer;
Hang spectral mirrors within the shadowy
Calvarium of your marrow; first one
Reflection, then another, until the
Hemoglobin crusts of your bone gleam as
Starbright as Actuality, then
Look, & look again; stare like Domitian
Into the brilliance of that sun.

Know yourself;
Return beneath a white sail.

* Gothic, "Know thyself" as tattooed on the author. Thank you, G.P..

MILESTONE

There was that time when I was eight, when my mom entered my room to clean it after I had delayed for way too long. She found my sister's Barbie hog-tied naked with my shoe laces in the back of my closet, & my sister yelled "There she is, I've been looking for her!" & grabbed her doll & stormed away. My mom looked down, saying nothing, packing up my Lincoln Logs. I stared at the floor, my cheeks burning, regretting that I had not cleaned my room in time.

Remember everyone, clean your room.

H(A), A GENDER-NEUTRAL, THIRD-PERSON, PRONOUN IN ENGLISH

"A (ă) [ə] pronoun, obsolete or dialect [for [OE] Ha= He, Heo, Hi, he (Hamlet III iii 74)
she (it) they, when stressless, chiefly in S. and W.] ME."

"Ha, pronoun, ME. Form of He, Heo she, he, they."

Oxford English Dictionary, Third Edition, 1955.

Ze went to the orgy.
Tey went to the orgy.
She He They went to the orgy & she he they were there.
Ha went to the orgy & a were there.

English needs a neutral third person pronoun
for purposes of clarification—
for when we don't know the gender,
or for the non-binary.

Check.

CONVULSIVE JOURNEYS OF BEING, OF DEATH'S RIVER, OF SLINKY FULL-FIGURED VALOR

To not do demands no thought,
To not do squanders no effort.

Inertia, that bull-whip duenna,
Programs us from the bottle like
Mushrooms, like rocks, swaddling
Us down for our protection in Shelob-
Sticky, Don't-Do-It-Webbing, where,
Within our tradition's gulag,
"No" is the only default we
Will ever need.

Should I kiss? Don't do it.
Should I touch? Don't do it.
Should I feel? Don't do it.
Should I try? Don't do it.
Should I? Should I? Should I?
No, no, no,
Don't do it.
Don't do it.
Don't do it.

Here, the "moral", the "wise", the "respectable,"
Here, the divine sanction of Warrior, Priest, & Proletariat;
(Here, besides, the strong-armed blame, the dread, the disgrace.)

Over there, they insist, across the tracks, outside, far
Away & beyond beyond, resides every Wickedness,
Every Corruption—the dusk of Mordor, the balefires
Of Gehenna—nothing but pitfalls & snares &
Highway cannibals; don't do it.

Exhaustions of tears like waterfalls,
Oh we, our oppressors.

& Dear Fleshlings, all of this, when yet—when yet!
Outside, over there—awaits rhapsody in sparkly floods
Of love's intractable delirium—the barefaced Odyssey
Of Red Hilda; step on to Cloud Nine, Humanity,
Flaunt your bigger, better, kinder & higher self.

SCHEDULE PLANNING 101

"Groovy," said the flower kids
"Make love not war."

You have not visited Miss Mary Palm so far today
You have neither waxed the dolphin
Nor spanked the muffin—
Your coffee is yet unground

You have not traded treasures today;
You have neither kissed nor cuddled
You have neither given nor received
You have not contributed to your community.

It is not alone the dinner wine or candlelight
It is not alone the slippery friction,
The 3-dimensionals, or the gratifying skin;

It is the earthquake reverberations of lions & of tigers; the mad bellow of red deer;
It is the desolate wails of dire wolves;
It is the caravan from far off Xanadu bearing amber, acceptance & humanity;
It is the acid trip mammoth tusk, lustrous & coiled & snowy, which you stare at from inches away & feel & fondle for hours, saying over & over, it's so beautiful, it's just so beautiful;

It is gazing into another's eyes like the first transatlantic telegraph cable, locking hypothalamus to hypothalamus;
It is Houston, we have contact;
It is this, & nowhere else.

UNFUCK THE MAINSTREAM; NINA HARTLEY FOR PRESIDENT

The sundry Overlords of our Dystopia compete in their predation, hiding behind disparate brands of government & of business & of denomination, as if Grand High Poohbah titles glistened with anything but greed & irrelevance.

While scapegoating our mothers & sisters with whackadoo theocratic laws, these mobsters themselves enact forests of vengeance, cold-blooded acreage of felonious insipidity.

Xenophobic & harpy-ridden, they condemn the jettisoned transitioners & the rainbow fabulous for every evil, for droughts & potholes & unemployment;

These Hells Angel gangsters stick us with a mating display from the Twilight Zone; a long-winded racket in which they ravage our children while railing about "sodomy" & "fornication," while simultaneously wagging peanut shells to us rubes like back alley hucksters, knowingly shuffling pedo priests & pastors from candy store to candy store;

These moneytheistic Thuggees may don white hats & smile with babes, but x-ray the spin & behold Cortés & Pizarro riding neutron missiles like platinum thrones wrapped in Timur the Lame's crimson banner;

They declare themselves our socio-political liberators while endowing our lives with everyday harassment & sexual assaults, with bigotry & discrimination & criminalization, until we are left discarded, short-changed & pregnant & sticky from untested rape kits.

Rise up; sacramental masturbation is only the beginning; flash your mandrill blades, for we have bathed ourselves in dragon's blood & need fear no one; sex rights or Ragnarok;

Where parasitic brutality consumes, where compulsion & subjugation asphyxiate, let human esteem & goodwill prosper; let pamporia flourish, let shopping mall stripper poles & sex-o-ramas proliferate, let devotion & tenderness illuminate every blighted heart;

May a fleet of Holy Whores sanctify the Stratten Chapel of the new Playboy Mansion Vaticanum; let a glory-dressed Ms. Easter Bunny consecrate the crowds from the spring balcony of St. Anna Nicole's; Cicciolina for Pope!

Let porn stars become bishops, & prostitutes, priests; let suckling churches announce the Second Coming of the congregation;

Under Konarak's hallowed & naked banner, may love-offerings of Truth expose delusion's masquerade; let the insular surrender their fear & dare to leave their dens;

May flushed & orgasmic carnations bud from every Kalashnikov; may benighted deprivation fade into currently possible gratis wellness & college for all;

Kiss me now, kiss me forever, kiss & make it better; the bucket list of carnal needs consists but of bestowing pleasure; let fly Innocence, Exploration & Possibility; savor now & fake it nevermore; gratify, gratify, out from yourself; let fervor interweave us one to another, unto Gaia & the utter most;

May the caring afterglow of informed, full-grown, mutually willing & wanting orgiastic endorphins wipe clean the toxic smog off Fafnir's Stock Market, & may this empathy scour the sobbing halls of punitive Congress, & the dank & Oval, Ostrich Office, & may such human Wisdom exorcise again & for always the Pentagon Crips & Bloods;

May the Holy Barbarians of the revolution intone vulva canticles from every ziggurat, warbling melodic & ejaculate panegyrics that will burst apart the Magnum prophylactics of smallness & of hatred, bringing manumission, afterglows & solicitude towards everyone;

Let come sexual democracy; let ghettos of anatomy & of love & of other outcast labels collapse into irrelevance; let the cataphract of bighearted sensuality advance the resistance;

Let the jubilant moans of pornotopic liberation ripple across the globe like a clitoral tidal wave until the illumination of our minds balloons like taffy to the Oryx rims of the galaxy;

May disinformation wane, let the callow waken, let savage tabu wither away.

French the devil, join the outside; let empathy, honor & compassion dissolve your melancholic asphyxiation.

TAR PITS, WITH ICING

THE GOLDEN RULE OF LUST

My debaucheries are ecstasy,
Yours are quite hideous.
First principles,
ΛΝΛSTΟⅮΕÏNS
Anastodeins.

That is all.

THE GOLDEN RULE OF PORNOGRAPHY

Mine is erotica;
Yours is porn.
That is all.

THE GOLDEN RULE OF PORNOGRAPHY AS LEGALLY PROTECTED FREE SPEECH

Obscenity and Pornography Complaints Ombudsman -- Powers (3) The Obscenity and Pornography Complaints Ombudsman shall: (d) advise local governments about strategies to restrict, suppress, or eliminate obscenity and pornography in their communities.
—UTAH CODE ANN. § 67-5-18 (2010).

Free speech prevails inviolable, constitutionally protected, except for the free speech of pornography, where mean-spirited Puritans are gifted carte blanche to implement governmental persecution.

THE GOLDEN RULE OF PORNOGRAPHY & OBSCENITY

One is legally protected free speech,
Like opera or Dr. Seuss, but better,
(Depending on the whims of state law)
The other is not,
(Depending on the whims of state law)
That is all.

THE GOLDEN RULE OF OBSCENITY

Sexual imagery of children, or of
Adult non-consent
Are obscenity, illegal
In all fifty plus Puerto Rico,
That is all.

THE GOLDEN RULE OF OBSCENITY REGARDING CONSENSUAL ADULT BEHAVIOR

Mine is erotica;
Yours is obscene.
That is all.

THE OTHER GOLDEN RULE OF OBSCENITY REGARDING CONSENSUAL ADULT BEHAVIOR

That which possesses no smell,
Which cannot be seen, nor heard,
Nor tasted, nor felt;
Which cannot be dissected nor defined;
Which no science can detect,
Which can only be summoned
By invocation & psychic intuition,
Which only exists in books like Oompa-Loompas,
In Constabulary copies of Malleus Maleficarum:
That Platonic Ideal, that rarified ghost,
Yields prison & a lifetime as a sex offender.

No one agrees about ID,
Yet everyone knows it
When they see it.
That is all.

THE OTHER OTHER GOLDEN RULE OF OBSCENITY REGARDING CONSENSUAL ADULTS

When certain consenting adults hypothetically inform other consenting adults about the default settings of sex work or of abortions, or;

When certain consenting adults pop themselves off into intoxication via certain electrical devices, or;

When certain consenting adults knock at the velvet & slippery gates of Elysium with consenting adults not of their own race, or;

When certain multiple consenting adults slide their various units, respectively & all at once, repeatedly & with grand gusto, into one consenting adult's consenting cavity, or;

When certain consenting adults grind themselves into hallowed gnosis through a loving act of backdoor sex with another consenting adult, or;

When certain consenting adults affectionately kiss the genital gloriosa of other consenting adults; then, these & more are called "Obscenity," & every such a crime.

Who would require footnotes & attorneys for consensual adult human sex-joy? Winston Smith can tell you.

Obscenity is illegal & unprotected speech, it fails the Miller test*.
Oh no! It did not even study!

Obscenity lacks "serious literary, artistic, scientific, or political value"
Hooray!
Obscenity violates contemporary adult community standards
Hooray!
Obscenity is offensive to a contemporary adult with community standards
Hooray!

Gauge best the chrysalis road to sexual democracy by
The magnitude of howling from the Mahar old guard.
Outrage & offend, often & today
Steer us into sunrise
Hooray!

America, America, repeal your collective adolescence; nothing justifies unconstitutional decrees that jail consenting adults; Betelgeuse can sail between the knees of Human Rights, they are wide enough & giving enough for all;

The Supreme Court of Illinois said it bright when ruling in Village of Skokie v. National Socialist Party, "It is firmly settled that under our Constitution the public expression of ideas may not be prohibited merely because the ideas are themselves offensive to some of their hearers;"

Thus, in 1977, Neo-Nazi Stormtroopers gained permission to goose-step their way through Jewish neighborhoods populated with Holocaust survivors in Skokie, Illinois, because genocidal hatred is legally protected American political free speech, &

Because political statements of xenophobic murder are far more acceptable to the good citizens of America than the psychedelic marigold that is consensual sex,

Which subsequently ends up jailed like stray puppies in the obscenity cellblock with Vlad the Impaler, for American clocks gong thirteen.

*The Miller test as established by the Supreme Court to determine if media is obscene:
"1) Whether the average person, applying contemporary adult community standards, finds that the matter, taken as a whole, appeals to prurient interests (i.e., an erotic, lascivious, abnormal, unhealthy, degrading, shameful, or morbid interest in nudity, sex, or excretion);
2) Whether the average person, applying contemporary adult community standards, finds that the matter depicts or describes sexual conduct in a patently offensive way (i.e., ultimate sexual acts, normal or perverted, actual or simulated, masturbation, excretory functions, lewd exhibition of the genitals, or sado-masochistic sexual abuse); &
3) Whether a reasonable person finds that the matter, taken as a whole, lacks serious literary, artistic, political, or scientific value."
Miller v. California, 413 U.S. 15, 24-25 (1973)

THE GOLDEN RULE OF BOUNDLESS ILLUMINAUGHTY YOU

Boundless your mind & free your delights; you are a scholar & an accredited bibliophile, the unapologetic embodiment of the Private Case Delta collection.

Sybaritic champion, what is wrong with you?
Nothing. Nothing at all.

Confront the dangers & scorn the malicious,
For bloodshed hides within the shadows of silence
While Hope calls to you from beyond the fear.

Orgasm, that Columbus journey:
Permission is yours.

Think: permission is yours.
Speak: permission is yours.
Desire: permission is yours.
Civility; permission is yours.
Virtue; permission is yours.
Self-Empathy; permission is yours.
Repute; permission is yours.

Selflessness, the Rubenesque Golden Rule of altruism; permission is yours.
Truth, Honor's lodestar; permission is yours.
Acceptance Tolerance & Respect; the hominin feathered bed; permission is yours.

Shamelessness declassifies your Van Nuys self on high-five advertisements; permission is yours.
Permeating every locus in the universe simultaneously & throughout time; permission is yours.
Voracious vasocongested genitalic calisthenics; permission is yours.

Autonomy; permission is yours.
Unity; permission is yours.
The revolution; permission is yours.

Yippie!

THE OTHER GOLDEN RULE OF BOUNDLESS ILLUMINAUGHTY YOU

Every Desire calls forth Risk, the unjust cannibal god of retribution, a fiery berserker delivering rage & evisceration. Plague, pregnancy, miscarriage, trauma, morning sickness, death, abortion, arrest, prison, murder, morgue.

The punitive hammer knows no end. Women mirror Atlas, heroically defying all for genealogy, for obligation, or for a slice of Valhalla. We live only because a woman dared.

Read, then Risk. Put on your goggles, carry a sharp stick, & wear a seat belt.

FLICKERING WHITE

OVERCOME

Questing to overcome, Galahad the Acolyte,
Gorgeous voluptuary & All Things Possible,
Stumbles bewildered from the curtains, erased,
Unwritten, unformed.

Silence lays the bedrock of humility, the
Open-minded fever of a questioning Anastodeins,

Gracious BeautyTruth the four-breasted siren,
Flaunts her oh so hypnotic limbs; we sob in gratitude;
Lust delineates blindness, this I am & this I am not,
Inquiry, the questor's lance, sparks infinity from finitude;
Form, meaning & function effervesce prismatic.
David of Pellucidar, do you begin to understand?

Mother's heart, the Highest Conscience, fair compassion's womb,
Holds our I ams & our I am nots as royal twins alike.
Selfless & mammillary giving, oh baby, whisper-licks a
Fuzzy bunny trail like a maternal gush of honesty ink that
Divides away the cosmic gloom, my hungry White Rabbit,
We are more than the sum of our flesh; & O what flesh!

"NÏst saeÏ mag fraþjan swaleÏk guþ
Nist saei mag frathjan swaleik guth.*"
No one can understand such divinity.

Lethean streams flow me, pleasure commingles indivisible;
Exquisite orgasm, the auroral wellspring of tornados,
Of thee I sing, raving in Delphic hexameter, generous &
Gnostic; selfless glitteration devours molted skin.

Transcendence greets all, welcomes all, treasures all;
Loves all love, both foreign & domestic;
Come home, Lucius, chomp the rosy garland.

Skeireins 1:1.

SEARCH IMAGES: OF BUSTY REDHEADS

From one Humanity, attraction
Breeds a cosmos of aesthetics;
This het maiden chases pepper & dusk,
& that one golden streams.
This one glories in platinum blondes,
& that one in smelly feet,
& this one, this one only fucks in squirrel suits.
One taxonomy, yet one mutual, customary disgust;
We are the boogeyman, the terrifying Other;
Soar above small vindictiveness;
This is just first principles,
Transcend.

It is like food,
Or rather, our partialities of food.
We love this; we hate that;
The meal that delivers one to
Rapture nauseates the rest.
Everything is natural, it is all guesswork of
Junk & treasure, we have no manual to
Explain our appetites, no purpose,
No choice, it is like conch shells, or
Crossing guards, or static.

To talk about sex is not to sex.
Chase the Dao of your Way,
With civility & integrity.
Owe no tribute; collect none.
Squish apart liver & lungs & intestines,
Split marrow & fracture skullcap;
Batter upon the vacuum hush of your grave.
Try, define, & redefine.
Harm none, hate none,
Carry no guilt, bear no shame.
Unseen the Way appears;
Precious your own reborn,
Yummy & slutterrific,
Whorax Red Hilda self.

As the 1960's said:
"Do your own thing."

OF OMS, STARS, CROSSES, AND SHAMKHAT

Sleepless over years attempting to gratify
My own scalding cerebral emptiness, I chased
Enlightenment like that charismatic white whale,
Like those missing, Seven Gothic Cities of Antillia.

I suckled on the lupine teats of long counts & cuneiform,
I hunted in ashrams, trash cans, crack houses & tabernacles;
I reveled all night like High Wycombe upon the equine roads
Of Ulaanbaatar, I called the goodwill of untouchables my
Home, & Monad Brahman lodged in each alike.

Then one pyrotechnic, Fourteenth of July day,
I found it, my beloved El Dorado, subletting the back
Row of a porn theater in Dubuque—

Erato the time-roving völva weeping torrents of sex-joy &
Reassurance like Emancipation, who serenaded me with
The lavish empathy of bodhisattvas & of woodland
Nymphs, saying:

"Sacrosanct the symbols of Deity,
Sacrosanct the emblems of O Holy Flesh.

Sacred every portrait, every dick pic & every twat shot,
Sacred every stapled navel & every twelve-month bikini.
Sacred Maria Zambaco, sacred Red Hilda,
Sacred Aline Charigot;

Exaltation heralds the coming of Freya,
For multiversical the symbols of Spirit, & all alike divine."

AN AGONOUS LACK OF KNOWLEDGE

Creative are the first fantasies of youth, when one suffers the initial drumbeats of lust and limerance without yet a travel guide to the first mechanics.

Once in the 7th grade I awoke from a dream about a college woman named Claudia, who was the gymnast who stole the show at an exhibition I'd seen.

When Claudia first walked out, her eyes—her nose—her lips—her smile—her face—her ponytailed mane—stunned me, I could not believe someone so dazzling actually existed. Claudia's legs rippled like gilded honey, & her abundant silhouette shone lovely & lusty & proud. On the beam, her pirouettes slighted gravity, she was airy elegance, pure sunshine clad in sleek turquoise, tall & delectably hourglass.

It is when undying endurance quickens gloried muscle, when ripe womanhood bursts into satiny arabesques, that athletes bloom like panoramic cherry groves, & fleshecstasy hatches like the volcanic roar of a bullet train.

In my nighttime porn TV, Claudia had just thrown an awesome, long hanging Frisbee throw amidst the feral grumblings of Muscovy ducks at Crest Lake Park. Elated, I caught it with a one finger delay—when I glanced over, Claudia was gone. Her string bikini lay on the grass beside a palm; astonished I watched as Claudia crawled naked out of that thin red fabric—barely the size of a robin, she sported a furry tail like Wilma Little.

After this inexplicable whimsiness, Claudia returned home with me, where I fixed up a house for her in my room out of an unused birdcage, with a heap of hot pink cotton balls for a bed. Claudia rode on my bike wherever I went—night & day, we became inseparable. Claudia signed up for a university correspondence course to finish her degree in Fluxus Semiotics; each evening we worked concurrently on our particular homework.

Claudia was a godsend; she absolutely refused to wear any of the doll fashions I bought for her. "Clothing crimps my tail," she said, "Furthermore, I am neither a Barbie nor a Borrower. This metamorphosis became so that I would be seen."

Claudia went on to explain that her divine calling was to unveil that rongorongo mystery of mysteries, human female sexuality. To this end, she took center stage wherever we went, stroking off heroically & nobly & majestically. Claudia taught me the complex framework of her curves, kicking back wide like Annie Sprinkle while I gratefully listened & studied her through a magnifying glass. In this way, I quenched my own agonous hungering for understanding.

On that last afternoon, Claudia waited as always in my backpack during Biology class, but, instead of watching the filmstrip on paramecium, Claudia boffed a stubby pencil for the entire period. I was barely able to deflect this raucous event by scapegoating the room's pet mice, Romeo & Juliet, who squeaked frequently in their aquarium beside my chair. Thus began her final transfiguration into Godhood.

Claudia slept on the way home; concerned, I laid her on her bed. She did not arise by lights out; not until breakfast did Claudia again show herself, once more transmogrified, to glide around laughing, flying on stupendous, teal & purple butterfly wings. In that very hour, like a Lost Boy suddenly yearning to grow up, Claudia flew away to pursue a career as a librarian, because everybody is somebody's wet dream.

PHRYNE'S CALLA LILY S & MORNING CYPRESS KNEES

How many nixies can dance upon my aching eggplant head?
Every last lubricated one, hurrah.

At the initial rosy slit of dawn
My dewy Godhead rises like a stupa
To the jubilant sun, drizzling creamy
Blessings in showers of ravening hunger
Upon us all.

You are very welcome.

INFINITY

We are.

Urd Verdandi Skuld.

ISHTAR

Grokking eye to eye
Restore the ancient gaiety
that
you may feel.

O Ishtar
O violet gates
O to live & die in Babylon

That which isn't may yet become
ΛNΛSTΩϽЄЇNS
Anastodeins.

& LO, HUMANITY

I hope to demonstrate that a clear understanding of the principles of anthropology illuminates the social processes of our own times and may show us, if we are ready to listen to its teachings, what to do and what to avoid.
—Franz Boas, <u>Anthropology and Modern Life</u>

Before all lovely genital trademarks,
Before all clans or colors or totems,
Before all labels & other considerations,
I am Human, a sexual organism, a familial
Unity & an African great ape, equilaterally
Bound with chimpanzees & bonobos.

"I am human, & nothing human is alien to me,"
Wrote Terence the playwright, which is
Anastodeins, the Beginning;
To which I add—for we are Moonraiser's
Kids— "I am human; I am spectacular."

Each of us began as someone else's happy ending.
We inherit our splendor like an Olympic
Torch passed down to us during the bright
Kaleidoscopic light of sex & then

We are gifted out from the alluring
Deeps of our Mother—from between
Two nuclear self-sacrificing thighs

We are sex resplendent
Like compelling sunflowers—for
Sunflowers are sex
Roses are sex

That sticky yellow cum-blanket of
Pollen that covers my car is sex.

Antlers are fuck me.
The peacock's tail—
The long necks of giraffes—

The swollen red butts of baboons—
All all sex.

Flogging your darling with pussy-

Willows on Wet Monday—

Marriage lovespoons & the expected
Breakfast gifts of daggers & of broadswords—
Rubbing noses—pogo-dancing & fuck-me pumps—

Kissing loudly in the park groping in the dark
Roses champagne & chocolate
Hot tubs ballroom dancing tuxedos bikinis & beer

That kitten dizzy smile of all-night talks & possibilities
Love notes & reading poetry aloud
Holding hands & staring into irises

Passing perfumed letters
Waiting for the postman—the email
The phone call the text—
Risqué novels wine & song.

Sex the overwhelming
The Sanctity magnets of praline
Valentines & mushroom knobs

The shuddering knees
The sobbing in tongues
Sex the Junoesque carnalia of Anastodeins

The OH MY FREAKIN' GODS!
Thou
Art
Divine

Sex sweaty with any name or number
Sweaty on that sunset beach
Sweaty chained & flogged & fondled

Whip-cracked tied & paddled naked licking boots
Crying and moaning and screaming—
Because it always ends in screaming—

Sex delicate as a butterfly's perfumed caress
Sex ferocious as Grendel's booming clout

Sex the benevolent cement of devotion
Sex the puffy & receptive undercurrent—

Draped in black leather black rubber black fur

Corseted in purple lace & stuffed with dildos

Swinging upside down fucking in a tree
Dressed as Tarzan a sailor a hooker a fox

Whimsical & comical & profound—
Sex—nurturing & collaborative & significant—

Not dirty degrading or despicable not
Me against you or you against me

Not evil not thievery but

Holy in back seats back alleys back rooms
Holy on the sidewalk holy on the bed

Holy Holy Holy

SHOULDS & OUGHTAS

"Cindyaec—The ecstasy of being one's-self, of being natural, of returning to one's natural state."
—Nailucwis maxim from the Taazhpuur.

Hear the voice of Siduri.

Go naked among the
sweet-smelling pines, deep
in the tarpan groves where
the Forest Gods dwell,
where centaurs roar &
alligators rumble, where
erection anoles blaze aloud
their prayers & oak-tree nymphs
offer knowledge absolute
within the velvet of their
embrace.

Stand in the mosses
& ferns & cast appreciative
runes carved of orange
boughs; burn horse-cocks of
incense, coconut or jasmine,
give thanks, give thanks.
Light candles of remembrance,
sing your joy loudly to
the heavens,

Dance naked to the throbbing
rhyme of goat-skinned drums;
smile naked, kiss naked,
love naked, shop naked
vote naked, hold hands naked,
worship naked, naked hug the
Universe.

Just go native, it's the only way.

WE

Us the Great Wall around our hearts, our castles
Our DNA & our lemonade stands.
Us the laws that protect & serve,
The refinement the safety the civilization.

Them is across the line, the
Enemy, the Other, the rest.
Them no laws protect, no ethic
Delineates the outer bounds,
All is good all is right all is fair game;
Vermin merit no charity,
No safe harbor from
Murder or torture or extermination.

When this, the black breath of tyrants—
Madness & bile & wormwood,
Masks & base propaganda—for
None are Them & One & All are We.

LUST-LETTERS TO OUR SELVES IN SEVERAL ANATOMICALLY INTERWOVEN PARTS, BECAUSE THE CONNECTION OF OUR PARTS CAUSES EARTH-SHATTERING KABOOMS

I am not afraid to say it,
O dear externals, how I love you!
O dreamy grottos! O sweet cylinders! O rampant spheroids!
O toenails, O sacral Trinitarian lines, O calvarium!
In dumbfounded humility,
You are awesomeness distilled—you are astronomic;
We are delicious.

The prizewinning tulips of my love are Sennacherib's terraced & love-letter gardens of Nineveh, where airport marshallers deify my Illuminati pearl with vigilant intensity unto lush overflowing, all the while raving litanies in the syntax of centaurs to the Wonderland of my Holland Tunnel & I tremble, thinking of you, winged on the Technicolor rapture of my flamingo calla lily.

The satyr rod of my love is an unchained piston, the high obelisk of Great Zimbabwe looming over the vast & empty steppes, where those shaven, off limits nomads whose herds of stiff-maned ponies are as aphids to the gods, offer fragrant wineskins of airag upon rocky cairns in my honor & I swoon, thinking of you, grokking the silken granite of my spire.

Bioluminescent, we flicker like silver lame'
Pixie dust in the noon cheery sun.

I & I,
I
am
Infinity.

OF ELEVATION AND LIMBIC SYSTEMS

Lust, Lust, O scrumptious Lust—
Fly me away on the wings of sphinxes
To alien worlds under succubus skies
Where thunder resounds my enchanted
Heart & static drips from my tentacles
Boil my veins in longing & bliss & labial fire
Where Dionysian Madness sears my wanton soul Divine.

Like the famed Bell, except in reality,
Lust the fervent sixth sense proclaims
LIBERTY THROUGHOUT ALL THE LAND
UNTO ALL THE INHABITANTS THEREOF.

Lust umbilicals us one to another
The end of decadence is in itself
Pleasure is its own comprehensive reason for existence
O Holy Flesh, O wanton Muse I sing of your miracles
Severed and clunked upon a table
My head consists of mass & matter
It is a noun—a thing of bone & brains
& eyes & veins & muscle & of skin
I am a noun—a thing
My liver my tailbone my spleen
My dendrites my dandruff my corpora cavernosa—
The streaming iridescent software of my
Mind are all nouns, all things

Look at me
I am human—
I am proudly
Irrevocably
An object a noun a thing
Objectify me in your lust.

UNNECESSARY GIFTWRAP, OR, HOW THIS COULD GO BETTER

For many-titled Red Hilda; for Muffin, for Barbara LaFleur & the Bourbon St. antlered woman

Naked's a gift, a glory-bright magic
That spins clothing into crime,
& majesty into magnificence.

BIRTHRIGHTS

Liberty, equality, & the commonweal.
Food; water; shelter; healthcare; education.
Rock 'n' roll & extended aye-aye middle-fingers.
A private & confidential life.

Art Beauty & Truth—
Passion & Peace & Love,
Love the overflowing,
Love the rainbow lioness of nations—

Love & Freedom in flagrante delicto;
Boiling incandescent Freedom
Dripping Siduri-rhapsodic like a Qaraqorum tree.
Universal Declaration Freedom,
Freedom voracious,
Freedom, the love-root of Oh My Humanity!

ANY [PERSON'S] BUCKET LIST

To do the useful thing, to say the courageous thing, to contemplate the beautiful thing:
that is enough for one man's life.
—T.S. Eliot. *The Use of Poetry and the Use of Criticism*

Come Erato, come Siduri;

To breathe with the hunger of
The inferno;

To grapple with the Minotaur;

To fly like a Thunderbird across
Sight & sound & to return before
You have left;

To love lest the universe itself
Shall crash & cinder;

These, these, besides the rest.

NAILUCWIS LYTHOOTH, NAILUCWIS VIRTUES IN TAAZHPUUR

Cwislyn You & I are one, the world is one, all is one within the ourobouros of totality.
Daadyu Humility, self-effacement, put no one below. To be aware of human finitude & error is the start of wisdom.
Chaec No one is an umbilical-cord.
Maan-maan Everyone is necessary.
Maec Contribute, be able to feed yourself so as to feed others.
Thrictcaent Nonviolence, labia-heart, parent's love the highest.
Zool Whimsy, playfulness our rainbow effervescence.
Taartaazhaen Inventiveness, to grok the stream beneath the riddle.
Zaoth Sharing feeds, loves, & fucks, sharing gathers firewood, it hunts, it finds, it builds & cares.
Laerimlyn Gentleness shows respect, shows compassion, a parent's heart.
Gulyweegaen Cooperation, to join with for everyone, for everyone, for everyone is family.
Gaocanaen To talk, to speak. No one can stop another's tell.
Myluc Sex joy, intoxication in another.
Braoblyn To agree together.
Graetaen The wise never shirk an apology.
Thraihaals Each their own sovereign.
Eewoojishlyn Equality, all stand on the same toes.
Baarnylutaoc Trust the child to nurse when hungry.
Unszaoc Not-thing; things last but a moment.
Uuzhaecmourf Honesty, glitter-words.
Aantzuprushuth Courage, to be lion-horsed.
Baodh Frugality, use or eat every part of the alligator.
Taazhuthaarnain Perseverance, promiscuous-thorn.
Aarmao Mercy, compassion or forgiveness shown toward someone whom it is within one's power to punish or harm.
Misleeclyn Variety, differences are value.

NAILUCWIS NIPICLYN LYTHOOTH, NAILUCWIS CARNAL VIRTUES

Cwisos You & I are one, the world is one, all is one within the ourobouros of totality.
Nootucwis The finned worm-ouroboros who encircles the earth.
Shin The animating power of the cosmos.
Tsaoc The Teaching, the Way, the method of sexual tradition & explanation of shin.
Cindyaec The ecstasy of being one's-self, of returning to one's natural state.
Chicotai Manifesto, the coming out, the I am this & I am awesome.
Nailubaarmz Shamelessness, the goddess-breasted vanguard gift.
Bowin Life is not to exist, but to enact ourselves.
Oonaec Fearlessness, serenity, calm, inner peace.

Chaec Darling Vagina; a term of affection for all.
Soolyn Goodness, skill, intelligence, kindness, excellence, is a beauty that feeds shin.
Ourdoomtsoi Hospitality shares the familial embrace.
Huulths Graciousness, the continued, noble, effort to enable another's comfort.
Nuuclyn Gratitude like wisdom, sees beneath.
Taartaazhyow Compassion groks the human family.
Aamutain Inspiration catches & radiates like a mammoth herd, going where it wants.
Zool Whimsy sparkles our rainbow effervescence.
Zhaenzhaen Friendship ties the web & nurtures many hearts.
Heth The group puppy pile for sleeping &/or sexing.

Leeciscis Anatomy, to map the names & configurations.
Timic Body, a numinous realm of wonder with its own philosophies & entrancements.
Hiwith Pulchritude, our physical beauty, feeds shin; all of us are dumbfounding.
Dazhu Naked's a gift, a glory-bright magic that spins clothing into crime, & majesty into magnificence.
Dazhu Thours The Nude; artwork of a naked figure, the most respected form of art in Nailucwis.

Timicduumth Hypnotism by another's beauty. One can reach altered states by viewing another.
Cuuryltai A glittery meeting across the realms with other beings not from this dimension; transcendence.
Myluc Sex joy, intoxication in another.
Cwencwen One who is especially arousing, we are each another's cwencwen.
Dazhulyn Nudity feeds the world.

Plins A lap dance, an erotic dance.
Thoovyusoons Erotic dancer.
Waacaanlyn Taazhusoons Sacred whore, a giver, an intercessor.

Breec Hope gladdens our eyes.
Shuurguc Joy begins the velvet dance.

Aarnusaerinaec Lust, the requisite sanctuary of indulgence.
Aenposoons Masturbation, to know yourself benefits everyone.

Braob Consent, the first essential, humble, step of tsaoc.
Ugylys Communication, a message; one hears when others talk, one talks that others hear.
Lofuhow Listen, to "palm tree-hear"—listen with intent, with hearing as long as a tree is tall.
Roonu Mystery, a sense of awe & wonder
Naar Imagination, creativity's womb, multiplies the world.
Paart Play, role-play, sex, to make everything fun is tsaoc.
Lytowc Eye into eye, the supreme.
Wuunyaec Ecstasy.
Hucaa Two in one.
Aeglaaaen To Howl.
Aashodis Orgasm, the white light explosion.
Rel The vulnerability & giddiness after orgasm, an honesty.
Uuzhaecaen To shine, to glitter from within.
Lygaodhuuc Lovers weave fondness into orchids.
Zhoom Love confronts Tyrannosaurs.

OF PINK-RUMPS & SUPERWOMAN

Humbling you are, bonobos, but humans are the true erotic wunderkinds of the Great Apes! Who knew? Way back in the celadon days of tusk & tooth, we cranked up the amplitude of our frolics even more;

To everyone's surprise, some foxy dude gave up his salami bone for a fat & bendy anaconda, while some clever hottie chucked cyclic & pink-rumped estrus to the curb, trading up for top-secret ovulation & lustful virtuosity;

The silphium of carnality stood up clapping when sperm wars & nympho sex became the pillars for kith & kin, for tribe & state;

Beat that bonobos!

Furthermore, along the way, we gained a transcendent superpower; when ourselves we play, numinous & possible, some go other-where, astral soaring from the meat of us—we cross dimensions, we merge with the One, we call upon our gods & commingle with them;

Humans may be the copulation heavy weights of the Great Apes, but the fabulosity of the human female cannot be matched.

Even now, passed down from all those many years ago, women's marathon gasms dumbfound the lab coats; they try to comprehend, pontificating about "status orgasmus" or "Expanded Sexual Response," etcetera, blah blah;

The ever-rippling passion of Woman is the muscle of an avalanche, talk about potential;

Yet, it had once been held by many that female sensuality was only a myth not to be believed in, like Conservative kindheartedness;

Some of this originated at the Grand Opening of History, thousands of moonbeams ago & what a big to-do that was! Even before the champagne hit the bow, the mayor & his fellas met over martinis to hammer out new rules to go with their new civilization;

They decided that women needed to be deprived of self-awareness & of freedom in order to confirm their own paternity & to exert the social controls required for them to stay in power.

This also enabled the commodification of people, more commonly known as "slavery." More profit for them, score!

Though as genius as anyone, the new & improved women were deemed lesser than men, as pretty but dimwitted circus apes capable of amazing tricks like changing diapers & sweeping floors;

Women left their Monarch cocoons, wings clipped, for their new lives as mere incubators for the blessed patriarchal seed;
Not everywhere or everywhen, but in many & in ours & recurrently, women & their longings were anathema, were deviant—were suppressed for so long that people thought it impossible for a normal woman to even to want to feel fleshly physicality;

Society brainwashed women into agreeing that their own quivering swan-lotus, their own lovely clit—the only organ in the human body exclusively devoted to ecstasy—was a mutant deformity, a pale shadow of a man's far superior weenie, & better left always unloved.

When memory transforms in billows of acceptance
Pegasus resplendent you will lead the advance.

Anastodeins.

FROM THE DAWN OF MY SOUL SWEET MYSTERY OF LIFE OH GREAT OH LOVELINESS

Penis,
O penis,
Penis!

A ONE WORD LOVE SONNET FOR THE BEAUTEOUS, THE UNBELIEVABLE & THE SUBLIME

Vagina

HAIKU OF OVERWHELMING, QUETZALCOATL LUSCIOUSNESS

Fuck fuck, fuck fuck fuck.
Fuck fuck fuck, fuck fuck fuck, fuck!
Fuck fuck, fuck fuck fuck!

CONSECRATIONS

"Shake it Misha!"
—Sandy C., cheering on Mikhail Baryshnikov during the Bolshoi Ballet.

Nyla Claudia Roxanne
Brigitte Alicia Charlie Jennifer &
You; walk long & legendary.

Our need for our beauty is a rabid fury, a berserker ferocity;
From hammer to glans, every orchid shred of every one of us scorches
Off our eyes, consigning us to rhapsody in quatrains of Tunguska Rubáiyát.

Yet, awash in rancid self-loathing, those many-blinkered Sawney Beans choke upon the
poison ivy of their spite while barking out their tired line, that to look is a crime, to look
is adultery, to look is base lechery;

When our beauty celibates like daffodils or Victoria Falls.
All's a gift, whether hands or hair or labia,
Looking lusts not, loves not, cheats not;
It judges not, favors not, steals not,
Looking breeds neither jealousy nor insecurity,
Those bastard cankers of our tribe—
Beauty sparkles like an impenitent absinthe
Faerie waving her licorice wand,
Glittering the acrid smoke-stacks of
Forevermore Day-Glo, & with unicorns.

Or when our beauty salivates like a double cockstand wombat.
In the wildfire of our sight we send our minds to new worlds,
Role-playing the bump-&-grind Shulamite rampantly entwined
With her Solomon, that whirling dervish bull-dancer climbing
Those awe-inspiring coconut palms,
& in rapture we become; breezy, empty of self & anodyne.

Seize the beauty; seize the joie de vivre;
No guilt, no shame, no harm,
To look is to human,
Flesh, flesh, O glorious flesh!

Venerable pulchritude, bestow your gravid benevolence.

SUCCUBUS MILK

Curiosity begs input like heroin.
Altruism cuts off a hand for another.
Fairness shares the squirrel.
Generosity, because we breathe large.
Love & lust fling knotworks of doors & nationhood.
Cooperation, together benevolence.
Creativity passionately bangs Imagination unto the holy of holies.
Tool-wielding chimp, wheels, Sputnik.
Compassion the exospheric, grokking into kindheartedness. The more scars, the more that humans grok, suffering yields understanding.

Absent these in our muddiest, we are malicious, indifferent, demonic;
yet in our loftiness, we are like gods.

THE SUM OF WE

Enraptured I enwomb you—
ravenous for the incandescent
pumping bliss of you within me.

With every mystic, amaranthine taste
our skin flames—our atoms
supernova, & you &
I & all Existence fades in
waves of flickering white, &
I am you, & I &
I am white flashing light,
    & we are
        Infinity.

LAISSEZ LES BONS TEMPS ROULER

Frïiaþwa jah lustus, winna jah gawaÏrþÏ
Friathwa jah lustus, winna jah gawairthi
Laissez les bons temps couler
Love & Lust, Passion & Peace

I am Shamkhat,
Come
To exhilarate the world.

KukeÏ mÏk

Kukei mik

Kiss me.

MINI-CHAPBOOKS & ZINES BY THE AUTHOR

Scaff, Gregory. *The Abandoned and The Undead.* Annapolis, MD: Succubus Media. 2012. Print. OOP.

Scaff, Gregory. *Breast Clamps.* Annapolis, MD: Succubus Media. 2019. Print. Poetry Bite. OOP.

Scaff, Gregory. *Dramatic Theme Swells.* Annapolis, MD: Succubus Media. 2020. Print. Poetry Bite. OOP.

Scaff, Gregory. *Furball.* Burlington, VT: Succubus Media, 2004. Print. A poetry zine written completely in runes. OOP.

Scaff, Gregory, *Kettle Memento Mori.* Annapolis, MD: Succubus Media. 2019. Print. Poetry Bite. OOP.

Scaff, Gregory. *Nymph.* Annapolis, MD: Succubus Media. 2019. Print. Poetry Bite. OOP.

Scaff, Gregory. *Odin's Legislations.* Clearwater, Fl: Succubus Media. 1980. Print. OOP.

Scaff, Gregory. *Platinum Blondage.* Annapolis, MD: Succubus Media. 2014. Print. OOP.

Scaff, Gregory. *Poems, Prayers, and Curses.* Burlington, VT: Succubus Media. 2000. Print. Poetry Bite. OOP.

Scaff, Gregory. *Towards a More Respectful Language: The Need for a Neutral Third Person Pronoun.* Burlington, VT: Succubus Media. 2000. Print. OOP.

Scaff, Gregory. *A Taazhpuur Grammar & Lexicon.* Annapolis, MD: Succubus Media. 2013. Print. OOP.

UPCOMING

Scaff, Gregory. *A Taazhpuur-English Dictionary*. Succubus Media. 2025. Print.
Ed. by Scaff, Gregory. *The Book of Mark*. A Gothic & English Interlinear Edition.
    Succubus Media. 2025. Print.

ABOUT THE AUTHOR

Gregory Scaff was raised in Clearwater, Florida. He attended the Universität Wien and holds a degree in Anthropology from U.S.F. Gregory is a philosopher with interests in the cross-cultural evolution and history of sexuality, ethics, gender, and related topics. He is also a bibliophile, a conlanger, a poet, and an artist.

Gregory's Fantasy erotica poetry book, <u>Succubus Arts</u>, was published in 2023.

Gregory served as a consultant for the film *Conlanging, the Art of Crafting Tongues*, by Britton Watkins.

Gregory hails from a family of educators. He is a polymath who has taught classes & workshops in art, anthropology, poetry, medieval art, Gothic history, and on sexual rights. Gregory, as a longtime supporter for sex and body positive culture, is known for his poetic and artistic discourses on the body and the sublime.

Gregory frequents Mid-Atlantic poetry readings. His poetry & his Dada poetry has been published in *Obelisk Magazine, Circle Works, The Valley Literary Magazine, New Reality Magazine,* and in *Aequinox IV, Carpazine,* in *Rat's Ass Review*, and others. Gregory also self-publishes mini-chapbooks and zines of his poetry.

Gregory's paintings can be seen in Mid-Atlantic shows and galleries. He is an internationally known underground artist who paints mythic nudes and body-impression fleshographs in acrylic. With his art, Gregory Scaff is America's only Fine Arts artist of the gasm-impression. Inspired stylistically by the Fauves & Post-Impressionists, Gregory's motto for his work is "Uncensored Art for Uncensored Minds."

An art show Gregory participated in, was reviewed in *Newsweek*, December 13, 1993.

As an activist, Gregory has protested and marched for a variety of Liberal political, philosophic, religious, and sexual causes.

Gregory's own cave-girl constructed language, Taazhpuur, is online at:
http://www.frathwiki.com/Taazhpuur

Gregory Scaff's work has been collected in these esteemed institutions:
The Carter/Johnson Leather Library and Collection.
The Department of Constructed Languages Collection of the Austrian National Library.
The Leather Archives & Museum.
The Museum of Menstruation.
The Museum of Sex.

Gregory's work is referenced in the book *Women, Art, and Technology* by Judy Malloy, MIT Press: page 301.

When not otherwise engaged, Gregory hangs with his brilliant daughter and his Muse of a wife.

Peace.